SHEPHERD
OF MY SOUL

HEALING PTSD
FROM PSALM 23

SOKREAKSA S. HIMM

Guardian
BOOKS

Belleville, Ontario, Canada

Cataloguing data available from Library and Archives Canada

ISBN/LSI Edition: 978-1-4600-1330-4
E-book ISBN: 978-1-4600-1331-1
(E-book available from the Kindle Store, KOBO and the iBooks Store)

To order additional copies, visit:
www.essencebookstore.com

Guardian Books is an imprint of *Essence Publishing,* a Christian Book Publisher dedicated to furthering the work of Christ through the written word. For more information, contact:
20 Hanna Court, Belleville, Ontario, Canada K8P 5J2
Phone: 1-800-238-6376 • Fax: (613) 962-3055
Email: info@essence-publishing.com
Web site: www.essence-publishing.com

PRAISES FOR *SHEPHERD OF MY SOUL*

"If you want to know why the disciples of Jesus were not defeated by PTSD after seeing Jesus being arrested, humiliated, tortured, and killed, then this book can be said to be authoritative. The author is a teenage survivor of the Killing Fields during the Khmer Rouge regime. After his family was killed, he suffered from PTSD for decades. But now he has been completely healed by the Lord. He will teach you how to get rid of the negative impacts of PTSD in your life through meditation on Psalm 23."

—*Brend Ray-Sea Hsu, M.D., Ph.D., Taiwan*

A moving and profoundly insightful meditation on Psalm 23 by one who journeyed through the terrible valley of the shadow of death in the Killing Fields, where he witnessed and barely escaped the cruel slaughter of his father, mother, and siblings, emerging as a broken and deeply wounded orphan. Anyone who has read this story in the author's *Tears of My Soul* (Monarch 2003) and *After the Heavy Rain* (Monarch 2007) will be stirred and spiritually nourished in reading this book. I highly recommend it.

—*Jonathan Bonk, Ph.D.*
Research Professor of Mission Center
for Global Christianity & Mission,
Boston University School of Theology, USA

I had heard and read of Reaksa's story while President of Tyndale University. But it was only as Lily and I walked through Kokpreach village in Cambodia did we feel what coursed through his memory, with all its horror and loss. We saw the place where the young boy had untangled himself from the dead limbs of his family and friends and hid in the jungle.

Now, by this, his most recent book, I'm taken into the resolve of Reaksa's disrupted emotions, and with his understanding of the biblical Good Shepherd, I accompany the healing of his own heart and soul. In this reading, you will treasure insights that will lift you from your own shallowness, into deeper regions of a life where accompanying grace is both nurtured and liberated.

—Dr. Brian C. Stiller
Global Ambassador, the World Evangelical Alliance

King David knew everything about being a shepherd. He had looked after sheep since he was a boy. Only a shepherd knows what it means to be a shepherd. It's not an easy task. But in his best-loved Psalm, David became a sheep under the care of God, the Shepherd.

So also Pastor Reaksa. In this book, he becomes a sheep, looking to the Shepherd. He follows the Shepherd through green pastures and dark valleys—especially dark valleys! Those of us who have read his earlier books (*Tears of my Soul*, and *After the Heavy Rain*) will know how dark those times were. Yet God led him through death, the pain of loss, and the struggle to forgive.

As he shares with us his reflections on Psalm 23, may we also become acquainted with Jesus, the Good Shepherd, who not only leads us, provides for us, protects us, but most of all, gives His life for us.

—Rev. Dr. David Wong
Leadership Mentor, Finishing Well Ministries, Singapore

PTSD has become household-known terminology in recent years. Sokreaksa Himm shared his experience of PTSD and his recovery through the six meditative steps according to Psalm 23, and is witnessing the power of Spirit-led faith imaging, that forms a new spirit as a follower of Christ. Highly recommended for people who pursue deeper healing and spirituality.

—*Rev. Dr. Michael T. Lau*
retired Senior Pastor from LBC, York Region, Ontario

Reaksa Himm's *Shepherd of My Soul* is not a book of easy answers… but there is gold to be mined in his application of Scripture to the profound process of forgiveness and healing after extreme trauma. Reaksa, using Psalm 23, guides us through his struggle to be whole. He takes us into the gloomy rooms of Post-Traumatic Stress Disorder, all the while clutching the flame of Scripture which provides the only meaningful light of recovery in unfathomable darkness. He offers us a window into his calming meditative practices which reveal both his strengths and weaknesses, his victories and failures, on the long journey to healing. *Shepherd of My Soul* is not to be rushed, but rather carefully absorbed as a guide book pointing to freedom for those traumatized. I hope it is a guide and blessing to many.

—*K. Brian McConaghy, MSM, BA*
Founding Director, Ratanak International, BC, Canada

The journey back from major trauma is agonizing, and in some instances near impossible. How do you recover from the execution of your family by the Khmer Rouge in your teens? *Shepherd of My Soul*, an exploration of managing

PTSD, is not birthed from theory or second-hand experience, but from Reaksa's own life and pain—an account which he generously shares with us in the hope that we too will discover a Shepherd of our soul when we face our deepest sorrows and trauma. It invites us to face our pains in the light of Psalm 23, and in doing so, is a gift to us all.

—Dr. Brian Harris, former Principal, Vose Seminary, Perth, Australia; Director AVENIR Leadership Institute

To train the mind to be able to think like Christ, to re-imagine our lives to conform to the image that Jesus has of us, is key to victory in the Christian life. In this wonderful reflection on the Shepherd's Psalm, Reaksa teaches us all how we can do this, through meditation on the Word of God. No matter how deep the pain we experience in life, Reaksa's story and the training of the Holy Spirit tells us that we can all overcome. Thank you for pressing in to the Lord brother, so we can all learn this essential skill.

—Jeremy Denmead, Team Leader, Welcome Bay Baptist Church, New Zealand

In this extraordinarily honest volume, Reaksa Himm gives an extended meditation of how he came to see, to know, and to experience Christ as "the Shepherd of my soul." Growing into understanding this reality in many dimensions, contributed to his healing from the traumatic stress he chronically suffered following the violent loss of his family. Reflection questions after each chapter make this a valuable resource for individuals and for groups who seek to integrate understanding and addressing trauma with Scriptural reflection. It is a book to read in tandem with reflection and prayer.

This is a fascinating, disturbing, and hope-filled book. From the unthinkable horrors of the Cambodian Killing Fields to healing and freedom, the author describes how Jesus has walked him through the journey of recovery from PTSD. This is the story of how God's love rescued and resuscitated an orphan of genocide. It will give anyone who has felt broken by trauma hope that they can recover too.

From a good tree comes forth good fruit and *Shepherd of my Soul* is ripe, mature, spiritual fruit. From a man picked out by God for a very special journey, both of sorrow and joy, which has uniquely placed him in a position to experience much of what the world is now experiencing. For those who have ears to hear, this book will bring the healing touch of the Holy Spirit. It is a very timely gift of a loving God to His hurting world. In the *English Book of Common Prayer* (1662) there is a prayer entitled—"For all conditions of men" which reads: "Finally we commend to thy Fatherly goodness all those who are any ways afflicted or distressed in mind body or estate; that it may please thee to comfort and relieve them, according to their several necessities, giving them patience under their sufferings, and a happy issue out of all their afflictions. And this we beg for Jesus Christ his sake. Amen." *Shepherd of my Soul* is an answer to that prayer. This is Reaksa's happy issue out of his affliction, and also an offering of relief and comfort to the many who are in the midst of it, or who will encounter it in the future. May God richly bless the work and its earthly author.

—*Rob Medway*
Retired Headmaster, The Vine School, Hampshire, UK

This book speaks volume of Reaksa's faith journey. Even at the depth of his suffering he holds tightly to his Shepherd; he even refuses to become bitter with his family's killers; most of all he does not cut himself from his intimate loving relationship with his Shepherd. His great Shepherd had guided him through the dark valley of depression (PTSD) through Psalm 23, where forgiveness finally helped him to release all the unresolved grievances and bitterness.

—*Pastor James Lee*
Local Preacher of Faith Methodist Church, Kuching, Sarawak,
and founding director of Breakthrough Network Centre Bhd.,
Malaysia

Rivetted and mesmerized by the vivid descriptions of the tragedy the author had survived, my eyes were filled with tears and my heart was heavy as I read it through. And yet, it was such a blessed assurance that the Lord pulled the author together and continues to do so, by restoring his mind and soul, and welding his mind onto Himself and under His perfect peace. In his verse-by-verse reflection of Psalm 23, the author helps us see the grace and power of God in his own life and the lives of others. I am very grateful to this intimate sharing of the author's survival story of PTSD, just as the Shepherd leads his sheep. I highly recommend this book for devotions for an individual and a group of believers and non-believers, young or old, especially in times like the COVID-19 pandemic around the world. Thank you, Reaksa.

—*Toshi Sasao, Ph.D.*
Professor, Graduate Program in Psychology and Education
Director, Peace Research Institute International
Christian University, Tokyo, Japan
Fellow, American Psychological Association (Div. 27, 45, & 52)

Reaksa battled PTSD due to the horrors that befell him and his family, most of whom were brutally murdered by the black uniformed Khmer Rouge. This traumatic experience prevented him from living a normal life, until he met the Shepherd of his soul, as written by King David in Psalm 23. Through meditation, reflection, and the grace of the Shepherd, Reaksa found peace through the guidance and comfort of the Shepherd. This led to him being able to forgive his enemies with the power and strength bestowed upon him by the Shepherd.

In this book, Reaksa explains and guides you through the power of the Shepherd, and seeks to help those experiencing PTSD. Today, Reaksa walks free from PTSD because the Shepherd of his soul has healed and released him from this bondage.

—*Henry S. Wong, (Retired Rev.)*
Tauranga Chinese Methodist Church, New Zealand

*"The Lord is close to the brokenhearted
and saves those who are crushed in spirit."*

Psalm 34:18

DEDICATION

This book is affectionately dedicated to my wife,
Sophaly Eng,

my son Philos Reaksa Himm,

and my daughter Sophia Reaksa Himm,

and to the memories of my family who were killed
during the Khmer Rouge regime in 1977.

And to those who have suffered from PTSD.
This book is for you.

TABLE OF CONTENTS

FOREWORD

This book is a testimony for all people of all time. It is for all people because trauma is a part of human life. It happens in every culture and at every level of society. Those who do not personally experience such trauma will encounter, or must live with, those that have the traumatized. Most are not prepared for such encounters or do not even recognize the trauma, with tragic results.

I am one of those that did not recognize or understand post-traumatic stress. I am among the Mennonites that Sokreaksa refers to several times, a descendant of grandparents who escaped the anarchist slaughter and plunder in Ukraine, following the First World War. I cannot think of a more informative way to avoid my early ignorance than to read this book.

Jesus the Good Shepherd is an image that has comforted and enabled many because it is so appropriate to human experience. Dependence is the very essence of human existence and cannot be expressed better than the metaphor of being a sheep. The sad reality is many deny this truth. People like to believe they are self-sufficient, that the resources of science put them in control of life. This delusion only multiplies pain.

Sokreaksa has made a tremendous contribution to dealing with the monster of trauma. The worst deception is when science crosses over into faith, where it has absolutely no jurisdiction. There is a credulity to certain scientific explanations that is simply irrational belief. Human personality is not susceptible to being placed under a microscope. There are realities of mind and spirit that are more than a function of brain synapses. As this book asks so appropriately, "How do you scientifically measure the healing power of prayer?"

Sokreaksa leads us into the very real realms of emotion and spirit, which require faith in something other than human inquiry into testable phenomena. Here is a compelling story of a faith journey that leads away from indescribable trauma (no one can pretend to understand his experience) to a functional life, which has provided hope and healing in the very areas of the worst atrocities of the Killing Fields of Cambodia. One may not be able to speak of cure for trauma, but here is an example of the possibility of overcoming it.

Sokreaksa's faith journey has been through the lines of the Shepherd Psalm. I was knocked back in my chair to read his account of "preparing a banquet in the presence of my enemies." Forgiveness is at the heart of this story, but it was no magical solution. Sokreaksa used the words of Christ in preparing to forgive the killers of his father and mother in person: "Father, forgive them; for they know not what they do."

"I drew on every ounce of courage to repeat these words to my enemies. Many villagers were happy to see me hugging my enemies. My hope was that they had recorded in their hearts evidence of Christian forgiveness in this village. Tears kept rolling down my face. I had done the utmost difficult mission my Shepherd had called me to do. I imagined Him looking down at me saying, 'Well done, my obedient sheep! Bravo my sheep, you have set yourself free!' After forgiving them, I had my lunch with them. I brought bread from the city for my lunch. I shared my bread with them. I celebrated with my enemies. It was a joyful celebration with my enemy."

I once heard a bitter veteran, who had witnessed the atrocities in Hong Kong during World War II say, "I may forget, but I will never forgive." Shortly thereafter, I heard Sokreaksa say, "I can never forget, but I have chosen to forgive." This book explains the cost of that choice and its exceedingly great reward.

Some years ago, a church congregation asked that I recite Psalm 23 in Hebrew. Since then, a recitation of these charming poetic lines has been my prayer before sleep almost every night. I have pondered each phrase; I have had my own ideas about a banquet in the presence of my enemies. Those ideas have been transformed forever by this testimony.

Trauma for Sokreaksa only began with his escaping a mass grave where he was buried under the bodies of some of his family members and many others. He has even experienced trauma for showing compassion in saving the life of another. But at the end of this testimony I read, "Surely goodness and mercy will follow me all the days of my life." This might not be the phrase that first comes to mind to describe the life experience of this man. But he will have no other phrase be the summary testimony of the work of the Good Shepherd.

—Dr. August H. Konkel
McMaster Divinity College
April 2021

A Word of Appreciation

First of all, I would like to thank the Good Shepherd of my soul for His greatness, mercy, purpose, and grace in sparing my life during the darkest period of the entire history of Cambodia, when the Khmer Rouge ruled the country. My Good Shepherd has brought me on a long journey from the grave of the Killing Fields to Canada, where He gradually restored my mental health. Without the rich grace for my life from the Shepherd of my soul, this journey would have been impossible

I am indebted to my dear wife, Sophaly Eng, my beloved son, Philos Himm, and my beloved daughter, Sophia Himm, who have brought me great joy in life. They have given me the freedom to sit down in front of my computer and write this book.

I am also indebted to many good friends and prayer supporters: Cerintha Chia, Rebecca Lee, Emily Quek, Ramsay Chan, Dr. Brian Stiller, Ron Apperley, Margaret Gilligan, Layswan Goh, Stephen Fong, Neel and Pam Reynolds, Dr. Nancy Craig, Henry and Tina Dirks, Helen and Art Andres, Mark and Sandi Sandercock, Dr. Alan Kirk, Scott and Cynthia Veals, Erin Goh, Dr. Irene Ng, Grace Ng, Belinda Tang, and all members of Mount Horeb Presbyterian Church, Lionel Sloggett, Maggie Wong, Donna Stovall, Nath and Leath Uch, Kay Shepherd, Ian Shepherd, Graham and Jean Shepherd, John and Jeanes Frazer, Don Oates, Tim and Donna Kurtz, Tim Anderson, Darren and Minako Polischuk, Nancy and Jerry Davis, Marlene and James Macfarlane, Susan Beerman, Dr. Brian Hughsam, George and Carol McClelland, Glen Ong, SK Ong, Gerry Neal, Ken Crouse, Joe and Anna Teo, Stephen Teoh, Rudy and Doreen Wiebe, Steven Norman, Julie Pharshall, Ian and Carol Little, Alan Little, Ronnie Dawson, Carolyn Ulrich, Phil Ulrich, Dr. Sorpong Peou, Dr. Duc Nguyen, Thomas Chau, Ai Leng Tan, Tha Vann, and James Bo. I really appreciate their consistent prayer for my ministry in Cambodia. Without their prayer support I would not have been able to serve the Lord in Cambodia for twenty years.

I would like to thank Dr. Jon Bonk, Dr. William Craig, Dr. David Wong, Dr. Gus Konkel, Brian McConaghy, Dr. Brend Hsu, Dr. Luke Yeewen Haung, Rudy and Sharon Dirks, Dr. John Regehr, Tim Regehr, Dr. Grant Mullen, Ivor Greer, Phil Pharshall, Dick Stovall, Bob Kirk, Pastor Timothy Phau, Chuck Ferguson, Wayne Shepherd, Frank Beerman, Henry Wong, Joy Wong, James Lee, and David Martin, for making some suggestions for the first draft of my manuscript. I cannot find sufficient words to express my gratitude for what they have done for me. Finally, I would like to thank Gennie Kirk, Monica Murphy, and Jean Bonk for helping me with proofreading in the final stage of the manuscript.

PREFACE

Before I explain my motivation for writing this book, allow me to paint a glimpse of my life. I was born in a big family of eleven brothers and sisters in the small district of Pouk, Siem Reap Province, Cambodia. I was a middle kid among my brothers and sisters. I was brought up in a Buddhist culture, where I learned to observe all Buddhist religious practices. My relationship with my parents and my brothers and sisters was very normal. Life was so happy for us. But this kind of happiness did not last long. On April 17, 1975, the Khmer Rouge captured the whole of Cambodia. A few days after they captured the country, they turned it upside down.

All city people were forced to go and live in the countryside. My family was forced to live in the village called "New Liberated village" in Sreysnom district. We lived in this village for almost one year. A few months after we settled there, we realized that we were not going to survive. We were not farmers, and it was impossible to build a self-sustaining community in only a few months with nothing to rely on. Later, the Khmer Rouge leaders decided to send us to live among the old liberated people in many different villages.

In early 1976, my family was sent to live in Thlok village. Again, we lived in this village for almost one year. Then, we were sent to live in Kokpreach village. By November 1977, my family and other families had been executed at this village. I survived the execution.

In early 1979, Vietnamese soldiers took over Cambodia. In late 1979, I went back to live in Siem Reap city with my aunty, and I went back to school. It was impossible for me to cope with my psychological trauma. My study was not very productive, but I tried my best to pass middle school.

In early 1983, I joined the police force in Siem Reap city. By the middle of 1984, I had escaped to Thailand and stayed at Khao-I-Dang camp for five years. On May 15, 1989, I was accepted by Canadian Immigration and sent to Toronto, Canada. One year later, I received Jesus Christ as my personal Lord and Saviour and spent more than ten years studying in Canada.

In May 1999, I returned to Cambodia to lecture on counselling and psychology at the Phnom Penh Bible School until November 2002, at which point I went back to live in my hometown in Siem Reap, where I stayed for nearly eighteen years to build up the Khmer Christian Center (KCC) at Proyouth village, Pouk District, Siem Reap Province. In early March 2020, I returned to live in Canada with my family.

It was in early summer 2007 that I went to promote my first two books, *Tears of My Soul* and *After the Heavy Rain*, in Northern Ireland. My friends Alan and Ian Little helped me to set up my speaking engagements at a number of churches there. In the last fifteen years, I have spoken at many churches in ten different countries, but I have felt that Northern Ireland is the country where I feel most comfortable sharing my journey of suffering and forgiveness. In most of the churches in Northern Ireland, I could see many people were touched by my story. I could see people who were crying with me when I spoke. They usually came to hug me afterward and share with me how I had encouraged them to learn to forgive. Some came to tell me of their appreciation, and I often felt very warmly received by the people of Northern Ireland.

Others came to ask me to pray for them. In most of the churches where I spoke, there were people who would share with me their experiences of having at least one of their family members killed by bombs or guns in their country. They could feel sympathy for my loss and could genuinely grasp the meaning of forgiveness. I have spoken in many other countries, but I have not felt as comfortable sharing my story anywhere as much as I did in Northern Ireland. It has been ten years since my last trip to Northern Ireland, and I have received many invitations to return. I hope to revisit one day.

On one occasion, I met a man named John at a Presbyterian church in Lurgan. He was about thirty-five years old. After I finished speaking, he introduced himself and asked for my permission to speak privately. I was happy to do so and we sat down together in one of the prayer rooms.

John asked, "Pastor Reaksa, how did you cope with your psychological trauma? You went through hell in your life. I could never imagine how you have gone through so much pain, and yet you are so joyful as you speak. I listened to how you talked about suffering from Post-Traumatic Stress Disorder. What is the best way to deal with PTSD?"

I responded to him, "You ask some good questions, but it has been a long journey for me to walk. I wish I had enough time to share with you how I learned to deal with PTSD."

He said, "I went through suffering in my life, but it was not as traumatic as yours. When I was a teenager, my father was killed by the IRA. I saw how he was gunned down. I was so shocked. It has now been more than twenty years, but I still cannot erase these painful memories. I have a lot of nightmares and flashbacks..."

He continued telling me more about his struggle to cope with his psychological trauma. He had sought help from his church pastor, asking him to pray for him, but he still could not cope with it. He had difficulty falling asleep. He also mentioned that he was addicted to alcohol and his marriage was falling apart. He was so depressed and he could not keep a job.

After hearing part of his story, I did not know what to say. I wished I could offer some formula to help him overcome his personal trauma, but I did not have any such formula to offer him. I just sat down with him and prayed for him. I mentioned that I learned to meditate on Psalm 23. I briefly taught him how to meditate and how to focus his mind on the Good Shepherd.

After I left that church, I felt sad for John. I knew that he would have to walk a long and painful journey to recovery, and that he needed to have the help of mental health professionals. And, of course, he needed to be willing to look at his own brokenness and ask the Lord to heal him. Normally, people will seek out mental health professionals or else stay on a path to destruction. But for us children of God, He also offers inner healing. For God desires for us to be whole in spirit, soul, and body. That is the price Jesus paid.

My Shepherd chose this way to heal me to teach me many precious lessons. He is the Almighty God and uses various ways to heal and set us free. He has different callings for us, and He uses different ways to train us to impact a variety of people.

In several other churches, many people often came to me and asked me many questions regarding how I dealt with my psychological trauma. Some would ask, "How long did it take you to overcome your trauma?" Others would ask, "Did someone help you overcome your trauma?" "Do you have a scar on your back?" And more questions...

An elderly lady came to me after I spoke at her Mennonite church in Morden, Manitoba. She said, "You were a young lad. You went through so much pain in your life. I can never imagine what you have gone through. You are so special in the Lord. He took care of you." Then she went on to tell me about how her family had escaped from Russia. Her parents were killed while trying to run from the Communists. She survived and her aunt took her to live with her. She told me briefly that she had suffered a lot of nightmares for many years. She was in tears. She gave me a hug and walked away from me. I was, in fact, speechless. I sensed that she could not cope with her pain. I was not sure she would ever recover from her psychological trauma. In fact, I met many Mennonite people. They told me many similar stories of how they escaped from the Communist regime. I learned that most of these people had suffered from their psychological trauma as well.

When I went back to serve as a missionary in my hometown in Siem Reap Province, I met a good friend there. He was a retired soldier. I got a phone call from him one evening. He wanted to come to see me and talk to me. I did not know what his intention was, but I told him that I would be happy to meet him on Saturday morning. When he came, I sat down with him and asked him why he had come to see me. He said that he had heard that I used to help some people suffering from depression. He then began to tell me his story about when he was young, during the Khmer Rouge period.

One late afternoon, a few Khmer Rouge soldiers came to his house. He was hiding in a banana bush behind his house. His older brother was in the house. The Khmer Rouge soldiers arrested his brother and took him to the jungle. It was the last time he saw his older brother. He was very terrified when he saw his brother being taken to the jungle. He was very close to him. A year after that, Vietnamese soldiers came to Cambodia. He decided to join the army to fight against the Khmer Rouge soldiers.

Five years later, he was wounded on the battlefield. The Cambodian government sent him to the hospital. After six months he recovered, but he could not go back to rejoin the army because he was listed as being handicapped. A few years after that, the government decided to send him into the police force. After serving in the police force for about ten years, he could not cope with his diarrhea. He went for medical checkups with all the local doctors, but they could not find anything wrong with him. They could only suggest that he be careful with what he ate. He was very upset with all the doctors. Besides diarrhea, he also had trouble sleeping, and he struggled with nightmares. When he was awakened by a loud noise or the sound of gun fighting, he could not go back to sleep. Most of his nightmares were associated with his older brother being arrested by the Khmer Rouge soldiers. Diarrhea, sleep disturbance, and nightmares became his personal problems that he could not cope with. He lost his sexual desire. His relationship with his wife was not healthy. He drank alcohol every evening to drown out these problems. Eventually, he became addicted to alcohol.

As a Buddhist, he went to see Buddhist monks at the pagoda to ask them to pray for his healing from psychological disturbances and to receive a traditional water cleansing. This is a sacred ritual practice for cleansing from sickness, during which the monk would chant and pour water on him and splash it over his head to wash away sickness or bad luck. It did not help him get rid of the psychological disturbances in his mind. He did not know what was going on as fears, worries, depression, and nightmares controlled his life for more than thirty years. He had been suffering from PTSD. The consequences of untreated PTSD can lead to brokenness and destructive behaviour. For some, it is not worth living with such depression.

I got to know him personally, and I spent almost two years with him helping him to understand the impact of psychological trauma and how it affected his thinking and feelings. It took me a long time to explain to him how the trauma impacted his life and his behaviour. I also helped him to work through his unresolved grief. He was not aware how this was paralyzing his emotions. It was a bit unusual to see a man like him crying. Most men in this culture often believed that crying is a sign of weakness. All men who joined the army were trained not to cry. I was so grateful that he trusted me enough to open up about his brokenness. I was able to help him overcome his depression, nightmares, and fears.

After two years of counselling, during the last session I had with him, he brought his wife and daughter to see me, and they thanked me for helping him to walk through his pain. As I spoke with them, they told me that he had changed a lot over the last two years. He began to feel happy again. The whole family was very happy to see the change in his life. I too was very happy for them. What would have happened to him if he had not sought help? He might have fallen into the pit of personal destruction.

After spending twenty years serving in the small community church in my hometown, I came to realize that many Cambodian people from my generation have suffered from PTSD. Most of them have never received personal counselling or talked about their psychological trauma. They simply lived with untreated PTSD. In the Khmer language there is no terminology that can explain PTSD accurately. Most people who have suffered from PTSD just try to live from day to day. From my observation, I think it is very common that they deal with it by simply suppressing their feelings.

Now I am beginning to see that the younger generations have suffered PTSD second-hand. I am not sure that I can explain this clearly and scientifically. I have googled this subject and have found that there are some studies on how the emotional consequences of trauma can be passed on to the next generation. There is a possibility that the emotional consequences of trauma can be transferred to the next generation through DNA gene expression that happened in the parents. I would need to do much more research, but I have learned that there are two key indications of the presence of the aftereffects of PTSD in the younger generation.

First, parents told their children what happened to them during the Khmer Rouge period when the children were too young to really understand. Believe it or not, most of the younger generation did not believe what they were told about what happened during the Khmer Rouge regime. What their parents told them was beyond their understanding. It seemed so unreal to them. But some young people were affected by what they had heard from their parents. Most of the parents who suffered from PTSD lacked an understanding of psychological trauma. When they recounted their traumatic events to their children, they just spoke from their hearts, but the traumatic events profoundly affected the younger generation.

Second, the PTSD sufferers did not know where to seek help. These untreated victims of PTSD created a cycle of psychological trauma within their families. Most men who had suffered from PTSD would become friends with alcohol. It is a bit sad to say, but drinking alcohol is a social norm in this society. Worst of all, most men who suffered from PTSD would drink too much. They drank to suppress their pain and the memories of the psychologically traumatic events. Alcohol helped them sleep, or it helped them forget their trauma, but the consequence of excessive drinking created another form of psychological violence within the families. Children of younger generations would become traumatized by their parents' behaviour.

Due to social stigma, people in this culture do not talk about their personal psychological problems. They do not want to be labelled as having mental issues. Another factor is the lack of understanding of the scientific evidence of psychological trauma in society. When they have problems with psychological trauma, they simply do not know what to do.

Some of the most common effects of untreated trauma include family violence, suicidal thoughts, substance abuse, alcoholism, sexual problems, inability to maintain healthy close relationships or choose inappropriate friendships, hostility, constant arguments with loved ones, social withdrawal, constant feelings of being threatened, self-destructive behaviours, impulsive behaviours, uncontrollable reactive thoughts, and inability to make healthy occupational or lifestyle choices. These lead to feelings of depression, shame, hopelessness, despair, uncontrolled or irrational anger, feeling as though one is permanently damaged, compulsive behavioural patterns, and more. I have seen many Cambodian men, especially those of the older generation, have these problems. An addiction to alcohol is a common problem. I have personally experienced some of these problems. It took me many years to overcome them. It was a long journey for me.

My life was tossed up and down by my emotional and psychological trauma. I went through a lot of emotional and psychological disturbances and felt I was doomed to deep, dark depression. At one point, I thought that life was not worth living and I could not see any hope for my life. It took me many years to try to overcome my flashbacks, nightmares, depression, and fears.

When I wrote my first book, *Tears of my Soul*, I tried to put all the details of my psychological trauma into it. I passed my manuscript to one of my professors to read. After he finished reading it, he made a good suggestion. He suggested I should write a separate book on how I learned to deal with my PTSD. He noted that if I put all the details of how I dealt with PTSD into my first book, it would distract the readers from the story I was trying to tell. I took my manuscript back from him and deleted some parts in which I dealt with PTSD. I took his suggestion seriously, making lots of changes. I rewrote it, making sure that when people read it, they would not want to put it down. They would want to know what would happen next. I left the part of how I dealt with PTSD in a silent place.

A few years later, I wrote a paper based on my personal experiences of using the Bible as my therapeutic approach in dealing with the effects of psychological trauma, such as nightmares, flashbacks, depression, and fears. I wrote in detail how I meditated on Scripture to help me overcome them. I got my paper back from my professor. She wrote, "I respect your idea and your approach and how you use your Scripture and your prayer to deal with your PTSD, but you need to have concrete scientific evidence to support your argument."

I was stunned with this comment. How could I find scientific evidence of prayer's healing power to support my argument? I spent a few years trying to thoroughly dig out the concept of prayer and healing based on scientific evidence. I still cannot find concrete scientific evidence to support my argument, but I can simply conclude that my Good Shepherd healed my brokenness. This is a mystery of healing grace beyond scientific explanation. Science cannot answer all spiritual healing. In fact, I am not writing a scientific journal; this is my personal testimony of healing and a life-transforming experience.

Although I was very disappointed with her comment, I realized that the biblical approach never married well with the secular school of thought. These are two different disciplines in two different fields. The school of behavioural science is in conflict with the biblical school. It is impossible to marry the religious school with the secular school. How do I find scientific evidence to support my biblical argument? I left my idea in a silent place again. I was not sure if I could find any scientific concept that would support my biblical approach to PTSD. Her comment stayed with me for many years.

When I was teaching at the Phnom Penh Bible School, a small group asked me to lead them in devotions. I helped them to meditate on Psalm 23. I invited all the staff to sit down and relax. I asked them to close their eyes and take a deep breath to fill their lungs with air; then, count 1, 2, 3 and release the air out gently; then, take another deep breath. They needed to repeat it again and again. While they were trying to relax, I invited them to create an image in their minds, visualizing themselves as broken sheep who need a Good Shepherd to protect them. I explained to them that this visualization was a tool of spiritual communication with the Good Shepherd. It is a very vital tool for communicating with the Lord, but they had to learn to practice it again and again.

It was difficult for them to learn to relax. It was hard for them to learn to discipline their minds, but they tried their best. About six or seven weeks later, two of them came to tell me that when they went back home, they had practiced what I taught them. It helped them to sleep better. They encouraged me to write about it in detail, so that they could use it to help themselves and others. Even though I did not have time to sit down and write about my meditation, I kept practicing it for myself. It helped me to deal with my PTSD.

This small book has nothing to offer you by way of scientific concepts. This is not a psychology book to deal with PTSD. It is a devotional book dealing with my personal psychological and spiritual warfare. I am simply writing from my own personal experiences as a PTSD sufferer. In fact, this book is no different from my first two books, except that here I have chosen to tell the story through the perspective of Psalm 23. In addition, I share more details about my personal struggle with PTSD. For each of the six chapters on Psalm 23, I have included a "Your Review & Reflection" section for your personal studies and devotions. These sections will help you examine any hurt and brokenness in your own life. They are tools to help you examine your heart by contemplating each question.

I hope and pray that as you read this book, you will learn to meditate and reflect on your own journey. For me, as an ex-PTSD sufferer, life after a major loss is a matter of learning how to cope with emotional and psychological crises and trauma. The more I learn about my own emotional and psychological crises, the more I become aware of my need to depend on the all-sufficient grace of the Good Shepherd of my soul.

My ability and strength are limited, for I am just a little broken sheep who needs to learn to follow the Good Shepherd of my soul who leads me on in life. I might not be a good and healthy sheep, but I constantly remember that the grace of this Good Shepherd is sufficient for me.

He is the Good Shepherd of my soul, and in Him I lack nothing. I learn to surrender my life to Him, trust Him, and allow Him to lead me to green pastures. I allow myself to be restored by His grace. I learn to overcome my fears. He prepares me to meet my enemy. He abundantly blesses my life. What more do I need from such a Good Shepherd? Only the Shepherd of my soul can heal a broken soul like me.

PUTTING MY PAIN AND SORROW TO REST

I n late 2018, I received an email from Rudy and Sharon Dirks. They told me they would like to visit me and my family at Siem Reap, Cambodia. We were very excited to receive their email. I had gotten to know Rudy and Sharon in 1990, when I was in my first year at Ontario Bible College, now known as Tyndale University. Rudy was a professor of counselling and in charge of the international students at the College. He took the time to get to know me and asked about my life background in Cambodia. I told him a lot about the civil war in Cambodia, but mentioned little about my family. I did not have the courage to tell him about my traumatic experiences in Cambodia. At that point in time, I could not trust anyone because I was just trying my best to suppress my painful memories. In fact, I did not have the courage to look at my own brokenness.

A month before Christmas of 1991, Rudy asked me, "Reaksa, what is your plan for the coming Christmas?"

It was a very friendly question. But to me, it felt like a big sharp knife piercing through my heart. I could not look him in the face. I was reminded of my first year at College. After the final exams, most of the students had their relatives, friends, or parents coming to pick them up for Christmas. I did not have anyone coming to get me. I was alone. As I looked through my dorm window, I could see my friends hugging their relatives and parents. I could not hold back my tears. In moments like that I wished that I had someone whom I could hug to ease the pain inside me. There was no magical moment like that for me. I was alone by myself. My family was forever gone from me.

Now hearing this question from Rudy, I felt a sharp pain piercing through my heart and soul. I could hardly answer him. He could see the emptiness in my heart. He could see my secret pain of loneliness. He could hear the heartbeat of my loneliness.

I found the courage to tell him, "I don't have any plan to go anywhere and I don't have any family to go to."

Rudy asked, "Would you like to come and celebrate Christmas with my family?"

I was a bit reluctant to answer him. It was the first time in my life I had been invited by a professor to celebrate Christmas with his family. In fact, I had no idea what Christmas and Christmas celebrations were about. I was just a young Christian who had just recently converted from Buddhism. I had never celebrated Christmas before.

I was a bit shy to go to the house of someone who was not related to me, but I said to Rudy, "Thank you for inviting me. I would like to go, but what do I need to bring with me?" I was just trying to be polite.

"You do not need to bring anything with you. I will come and get you from the school in the afternoon on Christmas Day so that you can spend time with my family." After that, Rudy and Sharon became my Mennonite family. I will say more about this in the chapter on restoration.

Many years later, we were very thrilled to have Rudy and Sharon coming to visit us. We could never have imagined that we would have the special privilege and honour of their visit. They had been praying for us for many years. Now they wanted to come to learn more about our ministry and, most of all, to support us. It was a thrill for our family. On January 12, 2019, I went to fetch them at the Siem Reap International Airport. As my usual greeting, instead of saying, "Welcome to Siem Reap," I said, "Welcome to the land of suffering." They were a bit shocked to hear such a welcome. But they just smiled and gave me a hug.

We took them to the guesthouse and the next day Rudy sat down with me. He asked me many questions about my ministry, and then he asked me if I could bring him and Sharon to visit the grave where my family members were buried. I was not able to answer him right away, but asked him, "Tell me the reason why you want to visit the grave. I don't think that we could get to see it. People in the village farm on it."

Rudy responded, "It does not matter about the grave, but I just want to go there to pray for the spirits of your family and other victims, to break the curses. It is not a Buddhist ritual practice. I want to pray at that place of death and tragedy for God to overcome the darkness, death, and curses that occurred there and in the whole nation of Cambodia from the dark reign of the Khmer Rouge, and over the effects of that darkness still evident now. God spared your life, and led you to Thailand, and eventually to Canada where you met Jesus. I also want to learn part of your dark history."

I took a deep breath. It was not easy for me to say yes. I was not certain about going back to see the place where my family was killed. I was not so sure I had the courage to relive the painful emotional and psychological experiences. It had been more than forty years since I left the graves. Many times I visited the village and the school that I built for the people, but I had never gone to pay a visit to the grave. The distance from the village to the gravesite is about three to four kilometres. For all those years I had never wanted to visit the graves. I never thought that it was important for me to visit them. It was just a landmark. Rudy and Sharon wanted to come along to learn more about part of the history in the countryside.

On January 17, 2019, we got up early in the morning. Besides Rudy and Sharon, two friends from Singapore, two friends from Canada, and my wife Sophaly, wished to make the trip with me. They had read my books and knew me personally. We had our breakfast and we prayed for our journey. We arrived at the Chonleasdai village and got out of our pickup truck. I showed the team the place where my family had first been taken after being forced from the city. When my family first got to this place, the sun was about to set. There were about a few thousand city dwellers and it was very chaotic for our family because we were not used to staying in the jungle. It was about to get dark, so we could not do anything. It was so hot. We could hardly find any water to drink.

I remembered that on that evening, our eldest brother and his fiancé were officially married and pronounced husband and wife. We brought enough food from the city and had dinner at their wedding party. It was kind of a sad wedding, but it was all we could do. They spent their honeymoon with us, sleeping on the ground. In the morning when they woke, they were shocked to find two graves near where they had slept on their wedding night. It seemed to be a bad omen.

I pointed to the grave markers where we spent our first night after we were forced out of the city. Every time I pass that place, when I go to visit the churches in the countryside, the memories of that first night are always fresh in my mind. I can never forget the place where my eldest brother was married in a field.

We then continued our trip to Chrouynean Ngoun village. It was the second place my family had come to after we were forced out of the city. I showed the team the place where the thirty to forty thousand city dwellers were forced to camp temporarily, before they were sent to live in different villages. It was a temporary stopping place for the centre of the Sreysnom district. When my family had gotten to this place and we set up our tents, it was packed with other displaced city dwellers, and there were no toilets and no clean water to meet our needs. It was very terrible for the city dwellers.

There was a small pond inside the pagoda compound. The water in this small pond was sufficient only for the local monks and a few hundred villagers. We took water from this pond to use. After the first week, the water in the pond dried up and we found the skeletons of the Republican soldiers who were killed in this pond. We learned that a few years prior to our arrival, this place had been a heavy battlefield between the Khmer Rouge soldiers and the Republican soldiers.

I also pointed out the Buddhist temple nearby. My father was once sent to destroy this temple. He told me that many former professors, teachers, and professionals had been sent to destroy it. They were sent to be tested. If they refused to destroy this temple, they would be executed. The Khmer Rouge believed that religion was a waste of time. Anyone who remained faithful in worshipping the Buddha statues during that time would be considered an enemy of the Khmer Rouge.

When my father arrived at the temple, his friends told him to do whatever the Khmer Rouge soldiers ordered him to do. Otherwise he would be killed. You can imagine how hard it was for my father who had observed and practiced Buddhism all his life. When he realized that he was being sent to destroy this Buddhist temple, he was horrified. But the fear of being killed overwhelmed him. He was left with no alternative. Destroying this Buddhist temple and the Buddha statues was like killing Buddha himself and his own soul too. My father told me that at first he was too shaky to break down this temple. He closed his eyes and asked Buddha to forgive him. In his heart, he wept and wept.

Many years after the Khmer Rouge regime was over, Buddhist believers in this village rebuilt this temple. Today it is a beautiful temple again. I could never imagine how my father had closed his eyes and broke down the wall of this temple. How could I ever forget this story about my father?

We continued our journey to the village. On the way, I pointed to two bushes where my two older brothers were killed in different places. I could not find their bones to bring back to the city because their bodies were buried so shallow that floods washed away their bones.

We arrived at God's Grace Primary School in Kokpreach. This school stands as a symbol of my forgiveness to the people here. Before I came back to Cambodia, there was no local school. After I came back to forgive the killers in this village, I raised funds from selling my first book and built a school for the people. Five of the kids who studied in this school more than ten years ago came from the man who killed my family. I also learned that one of the students who came to study in this school went on to study in Phnom Penh to become a doctor. My heart was filled with joy when I heard about this man. It was joyful to see change in this community.

We spent about forty-five minutes at the school. I asked the school principal to call all the students to line up. We distributed school supplies to all the students and teachers. Before we left the school, Rudy said, "Reaksa, I am so proud of you for what you have done in this village. I can tell that it would be impossible to do this with your own strength, but like you said, 'It is the power of the grace of God.' You have done great work in this village."

Then I led the team to the spot of my old house. It was a small house for our family. I stood on the exact spot where my younger brothers and a sister and I embraced each other on the day the Khmer Rouge soldiers took us from here to the jungle for execution. I could never forget that day. My hands and legs were shaking uncontrollably. My leg muscles had lost all their strength. I could not stand and I could not sit still. My younger brothers and sister were shaking with fear too. I could never imagine that the fear of being killed would be so terrible for all of us.

I showed the fence where my younger brother was hung and tortured. He was forced to confess that he stole two pieces of corn. I could never forget how my parents were lined up and forced to watch their son tortured in front of them. And how they lectured my parents. Every time I came to visit this place my heart was so heavy. The memories were always fresh in my mind. My brother was suspended on this fence. At one point he was tortured until he lost consciousness. One phrase they used to lecture us often rang in my ears, "If any of you steals like him, you will be punished like him, or we will send you to the school." After they tortured my younger brother, they unhooked him from the fence and hung the two ears of corn around his neck. Then they dragged him around the village.

I led the team through the road where my younger brother was dragged by the Khmer Rouge soldiers. They stopped in front of the new-liberated people to show them how much they hated thieves. When they stopped in front of the house, they hit my younger brother with a stick and forced him to say, "I will never steal again!"

We were humiliated to see how they used my poor younger brother as their object lesson, dragging him along this road. Many people watched my poor younger brother. At that time, what could we do to stop them? We had no power to stop these evil people. We were just victims of injustice.

When I first came back here, I walked on this road and I was filled with sadness. I thought these painful memories could never be erased from me. I think that many people in this village do not know the painful story of what happened to my family. I believe that most of the people who lived in this village during the time of the Khmer Rouge have died, and that many people in this village are a new generation or have moved here from other villages. I have walked on this road many times and I have met many people who have no idea what had happened to my family.

When our team reached my foster parents' house, I introduced my foster parents and we took pictures together. I asked my foster father, "Pok [father], can you bring me to the graves at Kok Ta-yoeung?"

My foster father looked so surprised. He asked me, "Why do you want me to lead you to that place? You have been here almost twenty years and you never wanted me to bring you there before."

I glanced at my foster mother. She was uneasy. She looked at my face and said, "Do you have the courage to go there?"

It was a good question. I felt as though a sharp knife was piercing through my heart. It had been more than forty years. I never wanted to face this painful memory. My foster mother kept looking at me, waiting to hear from me. It was not easy for me to answer her question. I looked at my foster father. He also was expecting me to respond to him.

I took a deep breath and said, "I just want to go there to visit the gravesite. These friends have come along with me to go visit that place."

I was not so sure it was the answer they expected to hear. My foster father asked me, "Don't you remember the place?"

"I am not so sure I could recognize the place now. Many trees have been cut down. I might not recognize the place. That is why I need your help," I responded.

I invited my foster father to sit in the front seat with me. Before I started my pickup truck, I said my prayer:

"Lord, the Shepherd of my soul, the Rock of my salvation, please give me strength and wisdom as my friends and I will make a trip to visit the graves of my family. I know that it is just a landmark of my family. It will be painful for me. I will relive the past history of my life. Father God, the Shepherd of my soul, I ask you to grant me strength to face the reality of past painful memories. Give me peace and serenity of mind to face this journey. It will not be easy for me, but I am ready to deal with my feelings. Please give me the courage to put my pain and sorrow to rest. I pray in the name of Jesus Christ, the Shepherd of my soul. Amen."

About ten minutes later, I arrived in front of the house of the man who killed my family. I came to meet him and forgive him more than fifteen years before. I stopped by to look for him. His daughter told me that he was not at home. He had moved to live in another village. I gave her some sausages, dried fish, and painkiller medicine. I said goodbye to her.

Then, we began to drive down an ox-cart trail. I remembered the day the ox-cart took our family on this trail. I began to feel sad. My foster father kept looking at my face as I drove on this road. He asked me, "Do you recognize this ox-cart trail?" "Yes, I know it, but most of the big trees are almost gone," I replied.

On the way to the graves, my foster father tried to talk to me about so many things. I remembered most of the places. I think that he could sense my emotional struggle. Inside my heart, I felt terrible. Sadness started to fill my heart and it started to pound faster. I started to pray, "Lord, the Shepherd of my soul, please grant me the courage to relive my past trauma. Help me to overcome my sadness. Please help me put to rest the pain and sorrow in my life. Lord, it has been more than forty years. Now I want to face those painful memories and have them healed. Lord, please help me smile again after facing these painful memories." My foster father kept looking at me from time to time. I believe he realized I was praying and did not want to disturb me.

We arrived at the old watermelon farm and got out of the truck. I showed my team around. Three days after my family was killed, I had come to this old watermelon farm that was being taken care of by two elderly men. When I first came to this farm, the two elderly men did not know me. They asked me, "Where do you come from?" I told them all that had happened to my family three days earlier. They thought I was lying. I mentioned their names, their children's names, and the village chief named Khmao. I told them how I survived in the last three days. They began to believe me, but one of the two elderly men started to mutter the words of a spell. I think that they thought I was a ghost from the spirit world. When they failed to make me disappear by the spell, they realized that I was not a ghost. I could tell that they were frightened. It took me a little while to tell them the whole story, but they found it hard to believe. After I finished, they suggested that I not return to the village because if I did, I would be killed. I did not know where to run. After that, they returned to the village. I slept at the watermelon farm by myself. It was a very scary place to sleep alone.

I took my foster father to see a large bamboo bush where I had lain down to hide near the watermelon farm. The next morning, the two elderly men came back to look after the farm. I also saw four *chlops* (Khmer Rouge secret agents)—

one of which was the man who killed my family—come along with them. They looked at this large bamboo bush near the ox-cart trail, but they could not see me.

I also showed my foster father a gate of the watermelon farm where the four *chlops* had again not noticed me. My foster father was so surprised. I used to tell him about this place. He had no idea until I showed him the exact spots where I had sat down. He said, "Your God protected you. He blinded them. You did not hide, but they could not see you. It was very close. But why didn't they see you?"

In fact, I did ask the man who killed my family about this when I came back to forgive him. I asked him how he didn't see me when they came to look for me at the watermelon farm. He told me that after the two elderly men went to the village, they told the whole village about my miraculous escape from the grave. When the four *chlops* came back to look for me, they intended to finish me off on that very morning if they found me. He could recall that he and his associates traced my footsteps entering the large bamboo bush, but they could not see me. I told him that I saw him looking at me. Then he and his three other *chlops* walked away from the large bamboo bush. It was a miracle that they did not see me that day. Otherwise, I would have been executed right then and there. My foster father could only conclude that it was my God who blinded them! I am grateful to the Lord, the Shepherd of my soul, for blinding them.

We continued our journey to the gravesite. My heart kept pounding faster and faster as we got closer, and my anxiety level was sky-high. My mixed feelings of sadness, discomfort, pain, and fear were boiling in my heart. My lips became frozen. A sense of uneasiness consumed me.

We arrived at the exact spot where the ox-carts had stopped. I relived the experience by seeing myself trying to get off the ox-cart while carrying my baby brother to my father, who knelt down to kiss the rest of us. I tried to give him a hug, but he could not hug me back because his arms were bound behind him. He could not speak. I could see the tears running down his face. I could recall the last few words I spoke to my father and sister moments before they were executed. They echoed in my ears. "Papa, I would like to thank you so much for being my father."

My father's response: "Reaksa, my heart is torn into pieces. You children are too young to die..."

My sister's words: "Papa, where is mother? I want to see her. I want to hug her and kiss her and say goodbye to her. Where is she? I don't want to be born like this again! I want to be born in another country where I won't see hunger and killing!"

My father was dragged to the grave, his last words being "It is time to die. I love you all!"

My younger sister said, "Papa, please help me! I am so scared!"

When I arrived at the gravesite so many years later, I tried my best to suppress my feelings so as to not cry, but I could not hold back my tears. They were running down my face. The memories of my father flooded in front of me. He was standing in front of one of the two graves. One of the *chlops* kicked his legs from behind. He fell onto his knees, and the *chlop* clubbed his head from behind with a hoe. My father was screaming in agony. "God help us! Help us, God!" I took my baby brother to the grave. I left him on my left side and someone clubbed me from behind. I fell into the grave. I could hear the screams inside the grave. The sound of the hacking blade echoed in my ears. I was overwhelmed with sadness. One last phrase I heard before I lost consciousness, "Don't bury them yet. There are more enemies to be destroyed here."

As I relived these memories, so many tears ran down my face I could not wipe them away. There was a tightness on my chest and I felt my heart was filled with pain. I recognized the spot right away. I pointed to the termite hill and a tree. Even though the graves had been converted to farmland, I knew where they were and explained to my team what happened that day when my family and other victims were taken to be executed at this site.

My foster father did not understand what I was telling my friends in English. He asked me to tell him how I survived on that day. I took my time to clearly give him the details. The one thing that captured his attention the most was the story of the bird that led me to the east side of the grave. While waiting on the *chlops* to return to finish me off, I was lying amongst dead bodies. I saw a bird singing in a tree. I pointed out this tree. It had been more than forty years and the tree was still there. I remember being so angry at the bird. It was singing peacefully, while I was lying on the dead bodies of my family and other victims. I felt as though I wanted the bird to disappear from me. I was so angry at the bird.

I picked up a piece of wood and threw it at the bird. The bird flew to the east side of the grave. I aimed at that tree. Then the bird came back. I chased the bird away again. The bird flew to the same tree. The third time, the bird only flew in the same direction.

You can see that there are many trees around this place, but why did the bird fly in only one direction?

Looking back, I strongly believe that the Holy Spirit sent the bird to save my life. If I had gotten out of the grave and moved west, I would have encountered the *chlops* who were dragging my mother and other women to the grave from the fields where they had been working near Keansrey village. After I got out of the grave, I went to hide in the bush the bird kept returning to, about 150 metres from the grave.

My foster father knew how I survived, but he had never heard the story of the bird making me decide to hide in the bush just east of the grave. After he had heard the full story of my survival at the site of execution, he could not imagine how it had happened, and he shook his head in disbelief. He said, "God chose to protect you. He chose you before you even knew Him. Without God's protection, there was no way you could have survived! No way at all!! I could not see how you could survive on that day. It was impossible. Your God is very powerful!"

I believe he spoke the truth. The Lord, the Shepherd of my soul, spared my life for a special purpose. My Good Shepherd, at His great cost, searched diligently for the lost sheep, the broken one like me, and He brought me into His love and Kingdom of Light. Many years later, I realized that I needed to respond to the offering of salvation from my Shepherd. I was absolutely lost. I accepted being found by my Shepherd. "Rejoice with me; I have found my lost sheep" (Luke 15:7).

If they had filled in the grave, I would never have had a chance to tell others the power of the grace of God in my life.

There were two graves. One grave was an old well. People escaped from the village to hide in this area during the civil war. They dug this well and they hid in this jungle.

When they decided to kill all the new-liberated people in the village, the *chlops* came to enlarge this well and make a mass grave. They also dug another grave near the old well but it was not as deep. When they took the people from the village in the morning (including my family, except for my mother, sister, and some other families), there were about twenty of us. All the victims were dumped in the first deeper grave. When they finished killing them all, they were not aware that I was still alive. They started to fill it, but I heard one of them say, "There are some more enemies to be added here." They left the grave without filling it in. I was in the first deeper grave among the twenty people.

I remember that thirty-three people (including me) were executed that day. Less than fifteen people needed to be put in the second grave, which was smaller. When they went to pick up other victims (mostly women), they left the first deeper grave open. The time they spent picking up other victims and coming back was, I believe, about two hours. When I was in the first deeper grave, I was covered with other victims. I waited there until I heard no more sound from the *chlops*. Then I decided to disentangle myself from the dead bodies. It took me about thirty minutes to get disentangled from the bodies on top of me. I searched in the grave for anyone else who might have survived. There were none except me.

Finally, I left the grave and followed the direction of the bird, which was on the east side of the grave. If I had stayed in the grave for about five to ten minutes longer, the *chlops* would have returned. I watched from my hiding spot and saw them dragging my mother, sister, and other women from the west toward the grave. I watched as they killed my mother, my sister, and other victims.

It would be logical to place the last group of victims in the second grave which was smaller. The first grave was deeper than the second grave. It should have been filled in already, but they chose not to. I never knew the reason why they did not fill in the deeper grave after they killed the first round, but I believed that it was a miracle of my Shepherd's mighty hand upon my life. It was the unseen, mighty hand of the Shepherd of my soul guiding my journey of surviving from the grave. My Shepherd's miracle was beyond anything I could possibly comprehend. My foster father was correct. He acknowledged that God, the Shepherd of my soul, took me as His child before I even knew Him. His way is beyond my understanding. This is a great miraculous story in my life.

After I related the details of how I survived on that day, all my friends and my wife were very quiet. They could not find any words to express the greatness of my Shepherd's miracle for my life. Emotionally, they were touched by my sharing and my tears. They chose to listen to my story and absorb it. As we stood on the gravesite, Rudy opened his Bible and read from Psalm 103:1-22:

> *Praise the Lord, my soul; all my inmost being, praise his holy name. Praise the Lord, my soul, and forget not all his benefits—who forgives all your sins and heals all your diseases, who redeems your life from the pit and crowns you with love and compassion, who satisfies your desires with good things so that your youth is renewed like the eagle's. The Lord works righteousness and justice for all the oppressed.*

He made known his ways to Moses, his deeds to the people of Israel: The Lord is compassionate and gracious, slow to anger, abounding in love. He will not always accuse, nor will he harbor his anger forever; he does not treat us as our sins deserve or repay us according to our iniquities. For as high as the heavens are above the earth, so great is his love for those who fear him; as far as the east is from the west, so far has he removed our transgressions from us.

As a father has compassion on his children, so the Lord has compassion on those who fear him; for he knows how we are formed, he remembers that we are dust. The life of mortals is like grass, they flourish like a flower of the field; the wind blows over it and it is gone, and its place remembers it no more. But from everlasting to everlasting, the Lord's love is with those who fear him, and his righteousness with their children's children—with those who keep his covenant and remember to obey his precepts.

The Lord has established his throne in heaven, and his kingdom rules over all.

Praise the Lord, you His angels, you mighty ones who do his bidding, who obey his word. Praise the Lord, all his heavenly hosts, you his servants who do his will. Praise the Lord, all his works everywhere in his dominion. Praise the Lord, my soul.

Rudy explained why he chose to read this Scripture. We had come to mark this spot, the spot that had witnessed such utter despair, horror, and death (...*the life of mortals is like grass, they flourish like a flower of the field; the wind blows over it and it is gone, and its place remembers it no more...)* with a far more powerful witness. The witness of speaking aloud the words of Psalm 103 in honour of Reaksa's father, mother, brothers, and sisters *(...as a father has compassion on his children, so the Lord has compassion on those who fear him...)*. We claim God's mercy, and shalom on the victims, the bystanders, and the perpetrators on that terrible day. We pray for a release from bondage and the gift of healing and salvation over the nation of Cambodia *(...the Lord is compassionate and gracious...)*.

God is not bound by time, circumstance, distance, nor culture. The eternal harmony and love of the Trinity—God, Jesus, and the Holy Spirit—is the anchor of the universe, the binding force that overcomes all evil, and the piercing light that extinguishes all darkness *(...who crowns you with love and compassion, satisfies your desires with good things...)*.

Our hearts are filled with tears and sorrow, mixed with sober reflection, and love and awe at the journey on which God has led you. You left this place in anguish and confusion, to return years later with forgiveness, healing, restoration, a family of your own, and a community of brothers and sisters *(...from everlasting to everlasting the Lord's love is with those who fear him, and his righteousness with their children's children...)*.

Then, Rudy asked me to read Psalm 23. After that, we stood in a circle around the gravesite. We held our hands and prayed to our heavenly Father for the release of the spirits of the victims. I started praying first, but I did not last long. I could not hold back my tears. Tons of tears poured down my face. Each one of our team took a turn praying over the landmark for a long period of time.

Now I stood in the place where I once made three vows. My tears fell onto the graves and I started my favourite song.

"Amazing Grace, how sweet the sound..." My tears overwhelmed me. I could not make it to the end of my favourite song—just a few lines and my tears kept pouring down. The team carried the song to the end. What an amazing journey! Now, I needed to look to the healing grace of the Shepherd of my soul. The place was filled with evil spirits, but now the sound of amazing grace was echoing in this place! I was filled with serenity. My sorrow and pain subsided with the sound of "Amazing Grace." My tears wiped away my sorrow and pain. The past painful experience was filled with the tears of joy, and the healing grace of my Shepherd. It was a turning point in my life. Now, I need to look to the Shepherd of my soul and rely on His grace.

Then Sharon started singing "How Great Thou Art." We all joined and sang with her. This place of fear and darkness was the deepest, darkest valley of my life. Now, the sound of "How Great Thou Art" echoed across the landscape. It meant a lot to me to have this song sung on the landmark of my family's graves. It was very painful for me, but I was able to put my pain and sorrow to rest after forty-two years. I returned home with a sense of release and relief. I could never have imagined that I would return to visit the graves of my family. I cried many tears, but I could leave the dreadful history, pain, and sorrow behind me. I counted this visit as the memorial and funeral service for my family that they had been denied for more than forty years. It was a Christian memorial service. It eased the deep sorrow in my heart.

I could never forget how, over forty years ago, I had knelt down beside the graves of my family to make three vows: "Family, as long as I live, I will try to avenge your deaths. If I fail at this, then I will become a Buddhist monk.

If I cannot fulfill my two promises, I won't live in Cambodia anymore."

I broke all the vows. I had an opportunity to take revenge for my family. I had a chance to fulfill my family honour, but I chose instead to forgive those who had executed my family. I had an opportunity to fulfill my second vow to become a Buddhist monk in order to pay gratitude and respect to my family. However I chose to follow the Shepherd of my soul, the Rock of my Salvation. I had an opportunity to live in Canada without coming back to this country again, but I chose to return to bring the message of hope, love, and forgiveness from the Shepherd of my soul to the broken people of this country.

After Rudy and Sharon returned to Canada, I asked them to write about their personal responses to visiting my family's graves.

From Rudy I received the following:

Dear Reaksa,

Thank you for taking us to visit your family graves. It was just a landmark of your family's graves, but the history behind it was profoundly painful for you. I think it was the jarring contrast that struck me the most. The beautiful, rustic scenery of the rural Cambodian countryside, of rice paddies, cows, and villagers contrasted with your story of oppression, torture, abuse, and killings that took place in this very same place decades earlier. It was as impossible to reconcile these two realities, as it is to reconcile light existing with darkness in the same physical space.

I had known you for over thirty years, had heard your story told, as well as read your books, and now we were driving to Kokpreach, the village where your family was taken, and eventually killed. It was a small group coming along with you. Over the course of the journey we stopped at various places on the way to the village, and in the village itself. You recounted your experience of some forty-two years earlier as your family was dragged from your city homes, trucked into the countryside, and forced into a harsh agricultural life, with no preparation, and no tools—only abuse, torture, and, eventually, death.

I had long looked forward to visiting you, Sophaly, and the children, Philos and Sophia. I feel close to you—sort of like an older brother. My heart broke to hear your pain when you first shared your story, and I feel such admiration for your tenacity. As you matured in your Christian faith and healed I felt so proud of you; of your marriage to Sophaly, such a woman of grace and integrity; and of the wonderful father you have become as you raised such quality children.

So, when we arrived at the village I felt a mixture of admiration for you whom God had clearly taken from death to life, as well as a profound sadness at the terrible events of so many years ago. The spiritual darkness of those past events was obvious, as was the residual emotional weight of suffering that you still carried. What was less obvious, and yet I believe just as real, was the continued effects of this darkness, both in Kokpreach village as well as in the larger national psyche of wounds that had never healed, relationships never reconciled, and traumas never forgotten.

And that was the significance, I believe, of our small band of friends of Jesus as we walked with you through your story, and ended up at the very place where your family had been killed and left for dead in the pit outside the village so many years earlier. The jungle had largely been cleared in the ensuing years. There were a few clusters of trees and the pathway that helped you and your foster father (the one who had taken you from the jungle into his own home some months later) to find the exact spot.

We gathered in a circle and I believe we were surrounded by a great cloud of witnesses in the spiritual realm. We simply testified to the redemption and healing God had already accomplished in your life. From a young Buddhist boy God called you into the Kingdom of Light and into the grace of God in Jesus. We prayed, sang, and read Scripture passages over that place of darkness and death; over that village of precious souls; and over the country that so desperately needs the redemption and light of Christ for the healing of the nation. We prayed that the grace and mercy and salvation of Christ that brought you as a young boy into the Kingdom would also in some way have reached your family that long-ago morning in that seemingly God-forsaken place—which, as it has turned out, was not so God-forsaken after all.

We understand that our battle is not against flesh and blood. And so, as Elisha prayed for his servant's eyes to be opened so that he would see the spiritual hosts of God, we also prayed for the eyes of the Cambodian people to be opened to see the healing, forgiving redemption of God and the Light of Christ which overcomes all darkness. So, while your story of suffering is profound, the still more profound reality is the healing and redemption you have, and continue to know, through Christ. It is this more profound reality that we pray into the generations of your and Sophaly's family, the generations of the people of Cambodia, and into the generations of all people who suffer in darkness—that the light of Christ would come like the dawn, with healing on its wings.

As I reflect not only on your story, but also on my own, I know that death, suffering, loss, darkness, and yet also healing, redemption, and life are part of each of our lives. In three decades of counselling, teaching, pastoring, and mentoring I have seen this in countless lives. And in my own life, I have experienced all of these. There is no comparing suffering or healing. The details of every life differ, and only God understands the depth of every human soul, and the sins, wounds, bondages, and strongholds that need forgiving, healing, unbinding, and freeing in my own personal experience, as well as in the lives of those with whom I've worked.

I have come to appreciate the different ways that God brings healing into our lives. Medical products and procedures have their place. Sharing one's story is core to psychological healing. And inner healing prayers for negative generational patterns, and spiritual healing for trauma, are crucial too.

I love you, Reaksa. I feel honoured to have you as a friend and brother, and to continue to walk with you and your family as your road of healing converges with mine. I bless you, Reaksa and pray for God's continued grace and favour on you, your family, and the ministry of forgiveness and healing to which God calls you to bless others through your personal journey.

Rudy Dirks

Sharon also wrote me her reflections:

Dear Reaksa,

"The fact that I could join you in visiting that place of terror and tragedy is a miracle in itself. You've asked for my feelings and reflections on that day, January 17, 2019, when you took us to the place where your family was killed. Even you had not returned in over forty years.

I think I had known you for a few years when you asked me to proofread your story. I knew some difficult things had happened to you, but did not know the extent of the trauma you had endured until I read your manuscript. It was unbelievable. And yet it was not a surprise that such horrible things could happen, because it was also the story of my people and my family. My mother lost her father and her grandfathers, many uncles, and most of the men in her village in the Ukraine when the Mennonites were persecuted. My people endured famine and imprisonment and political coercion much like what you experienced.

I never experienced any of the horrors myself, but have since come to understand the power of trauma on even the unborn. I have had to be healed from strange and irrational fears of things that I did not experience, but my five-year-old mother did. So, to be able to face, in a way, the very greatest fear I have had, was a tribute to what you also have experienced—the incredible healing power of God. I had seen so much healing in your life over the years, Reaksa, that it was a privilege to be able to share the visit to the graves with you on that day. You were emotional, but not despairing.

You were unwavering in your trust in God to carry you even on that day. You were careful to make the day meaningful, including a visit with gifts for the children at the school you built for the families of your family's killers. The healing in your heart was tangible—still you offered gestures of love and forgiveness to those who knew not what they were doing. You adopted the attitude Christ had. Your healing journey also begins with healing. A testimony, a model for us all. Taken from the life of our Lord, who did the same thing. We forgive those who have persecuted us. It's the only way to healing, wholeness, sanity, life, joy, hope, salvation.

In January we stood on the ground where you described the harrowing events of that day in 1977. It was appalling. It was evil. And yet, seeing you stand there, hand in hand with your beautiful wife, Sophaly, the symbol of your healing and your future of hope, it was not a depressing experience for me, but one of incredible beauty and redemption. You and Sophaly have brought Christ to the place where Satan thought he had won. Instead, we read Scripture and prayed in that place and it became holy ground. We sang 'How Great Thou Art.'

I'm not sure if I told you why I wanted to sing that song there. It was because we sang it at my dad's funeral. You loved Art Andres like a second father. When you missed his funeral last year, I knew it was very painful for you. This was a way of bringing your past and your new life together—joining with the 400 voices at that funeral, and another seven or eight at this holy funeral. Art loved that song and it reflected his love for Jesus, which you each shared. So, in January, we came full circle to honour the family that was snatched from you and haphazardly thrown into a pit without a proper funeral. We blessed them and prayed for them knowing that God transcends time. Together we helped you put to rest a piece of your pain and sorrow. It was an honour to do it with you.

Sharon Dirks

In fact, it was an honour for me to have my friends coming along with me to visit the graves. It has been more than forty years since I first left this place. Now, I am able to put the past pain and sorrow to rest. I never imagined I could ever have visited the place without their encouragement and support. It was a fantastic trip for me, a real turning point and a new beginning. I thank the Shepherd of my soul for sparing my life.

I love the Lord, for he heard my voice;
he heard my cry for mercy.
Because he turned his ear to me,
I will call on him as long as I live.

The cords of death entangled me,
the anguish of the grave came over me;
I was overcome by distress and sorrow.
Then I called on the name of the Lord:
"Lord, save me!"

The Lord is gracious and righteous;
our God is full of compassion.
The Lord protects the unwary;
when I was brought low, he saved me.

Return to your rest, my soul,
for the Lord has been good to you.
For you, Lord, have delivered me from death,
my eyes from tears,
my feet from stumbling,
that I may walk before the Lord
in the land of the living.

(Psalm 116:1-9)

THE BATTLE FOR MY MIND

Life after tragedy is full of psychological turmoil and emotional crises. It was a double tragedy for me. The first tragedy was my family being taken away forever. The second tragedy was that I lost my mind. The tragedy struck me when I was a teenager. I was not mature enough to handle the ongoing psychological trauma.

A moment after I regained consciousness, as a young teenager sitting on the dead bodies of my family, I could not understand what was going on in my life. Emotionally, psychologically, intellectually, and spiritually, I was dead—I could not feel, think, or reason. I was like a zombie. How could any young teenager handle such tragedy?

That tragedy struck my life on that day and stayed with me for many years. I thought I could never be the same person again. I had no idea how to cope with such trauma along with grief, depression, anger, and bitterness. I tried to run away from my pain. Nothing worked. Many years later, by the grace of my Shepherd, I learned to put the broken pieces of my soul back together one piece at a time.

Simply put, I lost my mind and the ability to cope with my daily life. During the day, I could not think properly. My mind became so disrupted by flashbacks—images of my family being killed appeared in front of me. Sadness and depression took control of my life and I had no joy in living. At night, my mind shifted from flashbacks to the fear of nightmares. I dreaded going to bed. It took a few hours of mental wrestling until I became so tired that I could fall asleep. And then my sleep was disrupted by nightmares. A few days after my family was killed, flashbacks and nightmares got stuck to my mind like super glue.

Up until 1985, in Cambodia, no one understood my psychological trauma. No one knew what was going on in my mind. For years my cry for help was not heard or was misunderstood. There were no psychologists, psychiatrists, or mental health professionals who could understand my mental and psychological state. I could not concentrate for more than ten minutes without being disrupted by flashbacks and fears constantly.

When I escaped Cambodia to the Khao-I-Dang refugee camp in Thailand, I continued to suffer profound psychological trauma, yet I did not know where to seek help. In addition to the psychological trauma I experienced, in the refugee camp, I witnessed another form of psychological trauma. I saw Thai soldiers torture many Cambodian refugees. Many Cambodian illegal refugees who entered the refugee camp without a UNHCR ID card were arrested by soldiers. They were dragged onto the road and tortured by the soldiers. These were horrible experiences in the refugee camp. Whenever I walked outside of my shelter and saw Thai soldiers, I froze. Psychological fears crept into my heart. I lived in the refugee camp for five years. I felt like I was living in hell. My mind was so restless. In fact, I could not tell anyone what was going on in my mind. Lack of general understanding of the impact of psychological trauma created the fear of social stigma. So, fearing people would think I was crazy, I tried my best to hide my psychological problems. One of the major problems for me was that I never trusted anyone.

Then, in Canada, I went to Tyndale University and took the Introduction to Psychology course. I realized I suffered from Post-Traumatic Stress Disorder. Based on the *Diagnostic and Statistical Manual of Mental Disorders*, Fifth Edition, by the American Psychological Society (DSM V), I met all criteria for PTSD.

PSYCHOLOGICAL SHOCK AND A CRIPPLE

I began to study how PTSD impacted my life. It took me back to that fateful day when my family was killed.

After I had regained consciousness, I tried to disentangle myself from the dead bodies. I was numb with shock. It was terrifying to see all the dead bodies in the grave. The psychological trauma inflicted that day would last a lifetime. I could not understand what was happening to me. I was seeing the dead bodies of my family in the grave. The psychological shock profoundly destroyed the core being of my life and my motive to move on. I became a psychological cripple.

While sitting on the dead bodies, in a state of psychological shock and disbelief, I cried out to Buddha. "Why has such a terrible thing happened to my life? Please help me out of this grave!" From that moment on, I felt as though my sense of trust was stolen from me. I felt absolutely abandoned, alone, and cut off from society.

A few days after my family was killed, I returned to the village to live with my foster father. One day, he asked me to look after his two water buffalo in the field. I decided to take them to graze in the field near the village. I sat down in the shade and kept watch over them.

Out of nowhere, a man named Hong approached me. I suspected that he would do something to me because my foster father had told me to avoid talking to Hong, that he was not a good man. Although I didn't know the details, I knew that Hong and my foster father had some personal conflict in the village. The moment I saw him approaching, I could tell that he was not friendly. I tried my best to ignore him, but I could not leave the water buffalo, so he came up to me and grabbed my hair.

He said, "I heard that your head was solid as a rock. I want to try to use my ax to see how solid your head is." I was so terrified, I could not say anything to him. He pretended to swing his ax at my head. I just closed my eyes and wet my pants in fright.

He continued, "If the *Angkar loeu* [higher organization] gives me an order to execute you, I want to know how hard your head is." He pushed my head to the ground and used his ax to chop the ground around me. When he saw that I had urinated, he laughed at me and walked away.

I was trembling and could hardly breathe. I went back to sit in the shade and wept for several hours. I felt so angry at the injustice done to me, but I was powerless. Fear took control of my life. I lived in the same village as he did. Every time I saw him I would run away. If I did have to face him, I lost control of my bladder. I felt totally crippled by fear.

Another incident took place when I unexpectedly met Comrade Hak. He lived in Romdeng village, which was about four kilometres southeast of Kokpreach village. He was one of the leaders in the region. I heard that he was the one who gave the order to kill my family and other people in the village. I had never met him before.

One day, I was assigned to bring fish to the youth mobile team in Kok Chombok, which was about seven kilometres away. That morning we caught a lot of fish. *Mear* [uncle] Thon and I went to Kok Chombok by boat. When we got there, we got off the boat to carry fish to the cooks. I carried two heavy buckets of fish on my shoulder. I walked in front of Uncle Thon, who also carried two buckets of fish.

Suddenly I heard *Mear* Thon say, "Comrade Hak, what are you doing here?" I looked back at *Mear* Thon and saw Comrade Hak in his black uniform and a red scarf. *Mear* Thon knew how I feared this man. He winked at me to let me know he understood. As soon as I saw Comrade Hak, I wet my pants. The fear was overwhelming. I felt as though part of me was dead already. I was absolutely terrified. I knew that he was the one who gave the order to execute all new-liberated people in my village. He was an evil man. I recalled that the day my family was killed, he sent his messenger to bring the message to my village chief to order the execution of my family. I rushed off to take the fish to the cooks in the Kok Chombok shelter. It was about five hundred metres from the place I met Comrade Hak. I gave the fish to the cooks there and quickly made my trip back to the boat by a different route. I got into the boat and fled from Kok Chombok.

This deep fear haunted me for many years and destroyed my trust in others and my ability to cope. I felt as though I belonged more to the dead than the living. I could not trust anyone. I did not know who I was. I was absolutely lost. I lost all confidence in myself and had no self-esteem. I believed I was beyond repair.

FLASHBACKS AND NIGHTMARES

I relived the execution of my family again and again. Most of the time, I felt as though it was reoccurring in the present. I could feel myself sitting in the grave on the dead bodies. I became paralyzed and could not resume even the most basic life tasks, because my thinking was constantly interrupted by these memories. As I scrutinized those years when I was struggling to move on from day to day, I can see there were two psychological battles for me. During the day, my life was disrupted by flashbacks. The cycle of flashbacks repeatedly played in my mind and interrupted any attempt to just think normally. The more I tried to concentrate on my studies at school, the more flashbacks would paralyze me. No matter how I tried to control the thoughts, they came back again and again.

After the Khmer Rouge government was forced out of the country by Vietnamese soldiers, I returned to live with my aunt in the city of Siem Reap. I told a few older people about experiencing non-stop mental and psychological torture. They did not understand and thought I was crazy. They would advise me to go to the pagoda to invite a Buddhist monk to spray water on me to clean my crazy mind. There were no psychiatrists or psychologists I could seek for help.

With the flashbacks ringing in my mind, again and again, my mind seemed to shift into the state of permanent alertness. I couldn't get rid of the fear that bad things might happen to me again. I seemed to feel the fear that someone was behind me. I startled easily. I often reacted to someone being behind me irritably. When someone was standing behind me, I would fear that I might be clubbed from behind. I often reminded most of my close friends not to speak or do something from behind me because he or she might get hurt.

When flashbacks attacked me during the daytime I would find it very disorientating. But at night, flashbacks shifted into the dread of nightmares. For years, going to bed was like hell. I could not fall asleep. Usually it would take me two to three hours to fall asleep. I desperately needed to sleep, yet the fear of nightmares made me miserable. If I did fall asleep, if any noise woke me up, I could not go back to sleep. I tossed and turned, or had to sit up until morning. I was exhausted the next day. I felt as though I was walking on the air.

If I fell asleep, I would see Khmer Rouge soldiers with black uniforms chasing after me or shooting at me. Going to bed was like a living hell. My heart jumped out of my chest and my body became sweaty.

I remember when I was in Khao-I-Dang refugee camp in Thailand, I slept with my friend on one bed with a mosquito net. I had a very terrible nightmare in which many Thai soldiers with black uniforms were shooting at me along the Cambodian-Thai border. I got away from the soldiers and I ran and ran. I did not realize that I had actually jumped from my bed and fallen onto the floor, pulling down the mosquito net with me. I had been screaming so loud that my friend, who did not realize it was a terrible nightmare, jumped out of bed and tried to run away. Unfortunately, this happened many times.

ANGER, DEPRESSION, ANXIETY, AND DARKNESS

For years after I lost my family I did not know how to deal with my anger. I did not realize the extent of the anger. I had been living with the longing to take revenge, which only resulted in anger, rage, bitterness, and no peace. The anger kept boiling in my heart and I felt I could not tell anyone about it. On the outside I looked peaceful, but inside I was full of hatred, conflict, confusion, and depression. None of my friends and relatives knew that I was living with such deep, dark depression. Depression was the deadly poison in my soul. It disrupted my way of thinking and behaving. I lost the joy of living. Every day, when I got up early in the morning, I could only see the darkness in my life.

A Cambodian way of expression about depression goes like this: "The sky crashed down on me every day. I could not bear to take the sky on my shoulder. This heavy load made my life not worth living." The joy of a simple day as a young teenager or youth was stolen from me. I was left with the difficulty of trying to concentrate and focus my attention on the task at hand. As a result, I would feel helpless and be overwhelmed by my negative thoughts. I could not erase these unwanted disturbances from my mind. They paralyzed my motivation to move on. It was just darkness for me. "The human spirit can endure in sickness, but a crushed spirit who can bear?" (Proverbs 18:14). How could I move on with a crushed spirit? I was so broken and my life became unbearable. At the time of my deep, dark depression, I could not see any hope of moving out of my darkness. I felt as though my deep, dark depression was beyond repair.

I felt as though my life was still overwhelmed by the sea of bitterness which enveloped me like a flood, and there seemed no way to remove it. I just hated the killers, and cursed them, and wished that they might suffer as I had suffered. I could see and feel results from so much anger, bitterness, rage, and hatred in my life. When this fruit took control, my life was full of misery. In fact, I was burying myself deeper in a grave of deep, dark depression. It dragged my life down to the point of meaninglessness. Every morning I got up and I could only see darkness. Hopelessness was my world.

After many years of living in depression, I could see no way to get out of the trap. The Bible says, "A cheerful heart is a good medicine, but a crushed spirit dries up the bones" (Proverbs 17:22). This verse reflects my life while I was living with deep, dark depression. Sometimes, I felt like I was swimming in the sea and could see no land or destination. I was lost and locked in hopelessness. At one point, I realized that the greatest enemy of my life was hopelessness. It was like what King David said:

Save me, O God,
for the waters have come up to my neck.
I sink in the miry depths,
where there is no foothold.
I have come into the deep waters;
the floods engulf me.
I am worn out calling for help;
my throat is parched.
My eyes fail, looking for my God.

(Psalm 69:1-3)

Many times in my life, I thought that life was not worth living. Even though I became a Christian, I was still living in deep depression. I realized that becoming a Christian did not immediately heal my depression and trauma. For me, there was no magical healing. I needed to understand the roots of my depression and seek healing grace from my Shepherd.

Many years later, I began to realize that my depression began when I was knocked down into the grave. It came out of unresolved grief, anger, bitterness, fears, anxiety, hatred, and self-blame. I suffered with depression for almost fifteen years. Let me put in a simple format the symptoms of my depression:

1. Feeling sad: I got up in the morning and could not see the joy of life. I just felt sad. No one could bring my family back. The sadness of losing my family stayed with me for years. I felt as though my hands and legs were being cut off from me. Psychologically, I felt handicapped.

2. Feeling of hopelessness: At one point in my life, I realized that hopelessness was the greatest enemy of my life. I could see no joy in life, but only darkness and hope-lessness. The valley of my life was so deep. This valley of darkness stole my joy of life.

3. Loss of interest and pleasure: I did not have goals or motivation. Every morning when I got up, I just wanted to have a very simple life. I was not interested in talking to anyone. I just wanted to be alone. I was not interested in any social life. I did not want to know other people. I was locked in my own world. I felt safe when I was alone in the room by myself.

4. Insomnia and no energy: Sleeping was the most difficult thing. I suffered from insomnia for at least fifteen years. I was so tired of wrestling on my bed every night. I could never get enough sleep. No matter how tired I was, I could not fall asleep. In most cases, my sleep was often disturbed by my nightmares. When I did not have enough sleep, I did not have any energy to move on. Most of the time, I was very weak. At one point, I thought that I could die of sleep deprivation.

5. Difficulty in concentration and absent-mindedness: I could never focus on my studies for more than ten minutes. My mind would be interrupted by flashbacks during the day. Sometimes when I sat down in the classroom, my mind would drift to frightful memories. I could not erase the traumatic events I had experienced. Sometimes I could almost hear the sounds of blades hacking away. There was no positive attitude in my life, and I felt as if everything seemed impossible for me.

6. Restlessness and bad temper: Because of the flashbacks, I could not stay still. My thoughts and ideas seemed to fly nonstop. I was living with the fantasy of killing my family's killers. I became restless and got angry very easily. Anything related to my family made me angry. When anger arose in my heart, I could not remain still or stay relaxed, and I felt I had no joy in life.

7. Anxiety and uncontrolled worry: Fear and worry seemed to be the dominant emotions in my life. I could not turn off my worried mind, which led me to think I would become crazy. A few years after I settled down in Toronto, I thought my life would end in the psychiatric institution.

The fear was very deep inside my soul. During the day, I was worried about everything. In the night, I was so worried I could not sleep. When I could not sleep I got headaches. For years I was addicted to painkillers, which I used to cope with my headaches.

8. Feelings of guilt: I had a constant sense of guilt after my family was killed. The consequences of living with unrelenting guilt was profoundly depressing. When the memory of my mother and sister being dragged into the grave for execution crept into my mind, I felt absolutely guilty for not being able to save them. This traumatic event surfaced in my mind again and again, and became my own psychological self-torture. I condemned myself for not risking my life to save them. Why did I survive while my family was killed? They were good people. They deserved to live, not me. I tried to rationalize why God allowed my family to die and spared my life. I did not deserve to live. It was not fair for my family. Many years of struggling with feelings of guilt led to self-blame and self-condemnation. This led to a sense of failure, and I believed I was a failure in life because I had failed to save my mother and sister.

9. Persistent avoiding: After returning to live in the city with my aunt, I made a habit of avoiding people I previously knew. I was afraid they would ask me all kinds of questions about the execution of my family. I did not have the courage to tell others how painful it was for me to see my family killed. Once, a friend of my late older brother approached me and asked, "Are you Reaksa who survived the execution?" I could not answer him. I just said, "You've got the wrong person!" It was so painful for me to hear such a question. Since I could not handle it, I tried my best to avoid him.

MY HATRED OF BLACK UNIFORMS

A few weeks after my family was killed, I developed a strong negative reaction to anyone wearing a black uniform. Most Khmer Rouge soldiers wore only black uniforms. The hatred for black uniforms took deep root inside me. It often reminded me of the terror I experienced during the execution of my family.

For years after the Khmer Rouge regime was over, I never wanted to buy black pants or shirts. Black uniforms instantly reminded me of the Khmer Rouge soldiers and my family's killers. When I escaped from Cambodia to live in Khao-I-Dang camp in Thailand, I had to face Thai soldiers in black uniforms. Whenever I saw them, panic and fear would grip me.

When I arrived in Canada, I was sent to stay at the World Vision Reception Centre in Toronto. The Centre hosted refugees who were under the Canadian government refugee sponsorship program. Staff at the Centre would help newly arrived refugees connect with their ethnic communities, find places to live, and find the resources to move on in the Canadian culture.

My first night in the Centre was shocking and terrifying. There was a young boy who came from a Thai refugee camp with my group. When he got to the Centre, he was very sick. His mother did not know what was wrong. Everything was totally new to her and she spoke no English. She just sat down and cried. The boy was so weak that he could not sit up. He could not eat. His mother tried to feed him, but he kept vomiting. When staff at the Centre realized his serious condition, they called an ambulance to take the boy, with his mother, to the Toronto Sick Kids Hospital. A doctor and nurses in the emergency ward opened the boy's shirt to examine him. They found his body was covered with red and purple bruises. They thought that his mother had seriously abused him, and they reported this to the police.

At about 11:45 p.m., someone knocked at my door. One staff member at the Centre asked me if I could speak English. They could not find anyone in the middle of the night who could speak English and Khmer. I agreed to help translate, changed my clothes quickly, and came down to the office. There were four Canadian policemen with black uniforms. I was so frightened. My heart was pounding so hard I thought that I was having a heart attack. My mind instantly went back to the Khmer Rouge. I felt frozen. I thought that they had come to arrest me. I had no idea what was going on. One of the policemen spoke to me, but I could not hear what he was saying. I looked confused, disoriented, and frightened. I almost jumped out the window, but I looked around and knew that I could not run. I tried to calm down, but my heart was racing like a frightened deer.

I said, "Excuse me, can I go to the washroom first?" I felt I was about to urinate in my pants. I rushed to the washroom and took a few minutes to calm myself down. I focused on taking a deep breath, and decided to return to the office.

One policeman spoke to me and explained about the Cambodian lady and her son, and they needed to know what was happening to her son. Then they escorted me to the police car and drove quickly to the hospital. Now, I was surrounded by policemen wearing black uniforms as the car drove through the streets in the middle of the night. Oh, my goodness, what was going on in my life? I absolutely felt traumatized once again! The moment I was in the police car, I was reminded of being driven by oxen-cart to the jungle for execution. I did not say anything to the police in the car. The terror inside me paralyzed me.

When I got to the hospital, one of the policemen led me to the office where the poor mother was being questioned by a policewoman. I could see through the glass window that she was trying to communicate with sign language. The mother did not know what to say, did not understand what was going on with her son, and why the police-woman was questioning her. She just sat and cried. I entered the room and I could see the mother's relief. The policewoman asked me what was happening to the boy. Why was his body covered with red marks and purple bruises? I conveyed the message to the mother. Then the medical doctor in the emergency room invited me to see the red marks and purple bruises on the boy's body. I was glad that I was no longer surrounded by black uniforms.

I realized that when the doctor saw the red marks and purple bruises on the boy's back, he thought the boy was being physically abused by someone in the family. I explained to the doctor that the red marks and purple bruises were the result of coining. Coining is a form of the traditional practice of *kors kha-yal* to cure illness. *Kors kha-yal* is a common practice in Cambodian culture that many Cambodians believe can scrape bad air and bring it to the surface of the skin to restore the body to health. It involves rubbing the skin vigorously with a thin metal coin. Traditional coining is commonly practiced in Cambodian society. It promotes a feeling of well-being. Coining also elicits a very basic physiological response: it increases blood circulation, helping to reduce fever, and relieves headaches and muscle pain.

The doctor was so surprised to hear my explanation. He went to talk to the police. I think they decided to drop the charge against the poor mother. I could see a glimpse of a smile from the mother after I fully explained the situation to her.

From that night on, I suffered from nightmares almost every night for years. I would dream I was being arrested by the Canadian police and sent back to the refugee camp in Thailand. Going to bed was like hell in my life once again. The nightmares felt real. In one nightmare, I found myself being chased by the Canadian police. I just kept running for a few hours. The police were shooting at me, but they missed me. I ended up at a deep Niagara Falls-like cliff. Behind me, there were many policemen pointing guns at me. I had no choice but to jump into the water. I was screaming so loud, I woke myself up. I fell from my bed. I was shaking. I could hardly catch my breath. It was a terrible nightmare for me. During my first two years in Canada, I tried my best to avoid the police with black uniforms. They reminded me of the Khmer Rouge soldiers. When I saw Canadian police, it triggered my psychological trauma and fears.

I will never forget another incident. When I was at Tyndale University, I stayed in the dorm. Students in the south wing of the dorm liked to wear black T-shirts printed with the school logo. They just wanted to be identified as the students from the school dorm. The south wing dorm leader, named Ian, gave me a T-shirt to wear. I was so angry at him for no reason. The hatred of black uniforms or shirts instantly erupted in my heart. I told Ian that I did not like the black T-shirt. He was shocked and did not say anything. He did not understand why I responded to him in a very negative way. Later, I returned to him privately and told him the reason I did not want to wear it. I told him of my painful experiences with the Khmer Rouge soldiers. Black uniforms or clothes often reminded me of the painful memories of how my family was killed by the Khmer Rouge soldiers. After hearing my story, Ian did not know what to say to me. I learned that the concept of hatred of the black uniform was born out of my psychological response to the traumatic experiences in my life.

> *He gives strength to the weary*
> *and increases the power of the weak*
> *Even youths grow tired and weary,*
> *and young men stumble and fall;*
> *but those who hope in the Lord*
> *will renew their strength.*
> *They will soar on wings like eagles;*
> *they will run and not grow weary,*
> *they will walk and not be faint.*

(Isaiah 40:29-31)

1

THE LORD IS MY SHEPHERD

*A call to surrender my life to the
Shepherd of my soul*

*The Lord is my shepherd, I lack nothing.
He makes me lie down in green pastures,
he leads me beside quiet waters,
he refreshes my soul.
He guides me along the right paths for his name's sake.
Even though I walk through the darkest valley,
I will fear no evil,
for you are with me;
your rod and your staff, they comfort me.
You prepare a table before me
in the presence of my enemies.
You anoint my head with oil;
my cup overflows.
Surely your goodness and love will follow me
all the days of my life,
and I will dwell in the house of the Lord forever.*

(Psalm 23:1-6)

One beautiful morning in the spring of 1993, I was about to graduate from Tyndale University with a bachelor's degree. I was thinking about my next path. What should I do after I graduate with my bachelor's degree? This question kept ringing in my head every day. I thought of pursuing further education. However, I seemed to have many problems regarding my school of choice, my finances, life, and more. I was not sure what I should do.

After finishing my counselling class one morning, my professor, Rudy Dirks, asked me if I could have lunch with him. I never refused such an offer. He and I went for lunch at the student centre. All around me I could hear the buzz of students talking about their education, their theories and perception about the school, professors, mission fields, and so on. I was not very much interested in talking about anything. I was hungry and just wanted to enjoy my lunch. I did not like to talk much while eating. Eating was always a serious business for me. My counselling professor had just finished teaching the morning session, and he was a bit hungry too. He just tried to finish his lunch.

After lunch, he wanted to get down to business. "I have finished reading your personal reflection paper about your life experience," he said. I just looked at him speechless. I was nervous about what was coming next. I wondered if I had done a proper job. I was filled with anxiety. He continued, "I am deeply touched by how you survived during the period of the Killing Fields and how you coped with it. I had no idea what had happened during those years in Cambodia. May I ask you some more questions?"

"Please go ahead, I will try to answer your questions from my heart," I responded quickly.

"How do you cope with your psychological trauma?" he asked.

The question hit me like an earthquake. No one had ever asked me this question before. It was not easy for me to answer. I immediately thought I should tell him that I was just fine and that I could handle it, so that he would not pursue it further. But that would not have been honest. I wanted to be honest with him. Then, I decided to face the truth in my life.

"I am not sure how I cope with it," I responded. My answer did not surprise him. He just looked into my eyes, the window of my heart, and saw the psychological distress in my life.

"What is the most troubling thing in your life?" he asked.

"I think insomnia, fears, flashbacks, and nightmares. Every night, when I go to sleep my mind seems to be restless, out of my control. It usually takes me three to four hours of tossing and turning before I get to sleep. Psychologically, it is terrible for me. I have never gotten enough sleep since my family was killed. Going to bed is almost like going to hell. I can hardly close my eyes," I responded.

"What else?" he asked.

I replied, "Every night, if I can sleep a bit, nightmares chase me like a shadow of my life. When nightmares wake me up during the night, I can never fall asleep again. My heart keeps pounding so fast. I get sweaty. I have to sit up for the whole night or wrestle in my bed till morning."

"How long have you been having these problems?" he asked.

I answered, "I think ever since the two days after I witnessed my family's execution. At least for more than ten years."

The conversation lasted almost two hours. He kept asking me questions; I kept answering him. At the end of the conversation, he made this suggestion to me, "Reaksa, I cannot imagine how you got through all this. I am not sure how you can cope with the nightmares, flashbacks, and depression in your life, but let me give you a suggestion to work through. Try not to run away from nightmares and flashbacks. Ask God to help you to overcome your nightmares. Read Psalm 23 or any Psalm that you prefer, and meditate on it. Imagine that you are a sheep. You need a good Shepherd to look after you." I was not sure I clearly understood him, but I tried to listen to him. Looking back on that conversation I had with Professor Rudy almost thirty years ago, I can see his suggestion paved the way for me to catch a glimpse of the hope of overcoming my psychological trauma. It has been a long, hard journey for my life.

Psalm 23 is very popular in many ways. The term "shepherd" is very familiar within Christian circles. I asked many pastors what the term means to them. Their answers mostly referred to God, the Father of Israel, or Jesus, the Son of God. In the Old Testament, the term "shepherd" is used in two ways. First, it refers to Israel's leaders. Secondly, it refers to the God of Israel.

As a leader of Israel, David was chosen by God to be the shepherd of His people. Psalm 78:70-72:

He chose David his servant
and took him from the sheep pens;

from tending the sheep he brought him
to be the shepherd of his people Jacob,
of Israel his inheritance.
And David shepherded them with integrity of heart;
with skillful hands he led them.

Moses was also referred to as a shepherd in Isaiah 63:11:

Then his people recalled the days of old,
the days of Moses and his people—
where is he who brought them through the sea
with the shepherd of his flock?
Where is he who set
his Holy Spirit among them?

The term "Shepherd" often refers to the God of Israel, in the Old Testament context. "Hear us, Shepherd of Israel, you who lead Joseph like a flock" (Psalm 80:1). "But He brought His people out like a flock; He led them like sheep through the wilderness" (Psalm 78:52). "The Lord is my shepherd, I lack nothing" (Psalm 23:1). In the New Testament, Jesus referred to Himself as a Good Shepherd.

"I am the good shepherd. The good shepherd lays down
His life for the sheep" (John 10:11).

Interestingly, the images for God used in the book of Psalms are very powerful distinctive metaphors. Psalm 18:1-3 says,

I love you, Lord, my strength
The Lord is my rock, my fortress and my deliverer;
my God is my rock, in whom I take refuge,
my shield and the horn of my salvation, my stronghold.

I called to the Lord, who is worthy of praise,
and I have been saved from my enemies.

Many parts of the book of Psalms are full of complaints. David expresses his feelings to the Lord in times of struggle, unfair treatment, frustration, confession, doubt, darkness, fear, anxiety, depression, and anger. Apart from the complaints, David also expresses his gratitude, joy, praise, and thanksgiving to the Lord. I personally find Psalm 23 full of comfort in many ways. In Asia, Psalm 23 has become very popular. I saw some young soccer players use this Psalm for their soccer jerseys, for their motorbike license plates, and so on. Some churches use this to sing the Psalm as praise in their churches, or read it for a wedding ceremony, funeral, etc.

I am not sure when Psalm 23 was written, but there are varying theories among biblical scholars. The theme of this Psalm seems to suggest that David sang this song when he was a shepherd boy, because he knew the relationship between the sheep and their shepherd. He poured out this Psalm from his personal experience as a shepherd. As a young boy, he knew how to take care of his sheep. He knew the dangers to them when they were lost in the valley. He knew where to bring them to the green pasture. Most of all, as a shepherd boy, he knew how to protect them from being attacked by wild animals. Without doubt, he knew by his personal experience the care and tender affections of a good shepherd toward his sheep. He had a lot of experience tending them.

The last three verses of this Psalm seem to suggest that David, sitting in his palace and looking back on his personal experiences, composed this Psalm to reflect how his life was comforted by the Lord our Shepherd during his flight from Saul and during some of his later conflicts with his own family circle and his enemies. "Even though I walk through the darkest valley, I will fear no evil, for you are with me; your rod and your staff, they comfort me" (vs. 4). And the Lord blessed his life. "Surely your goodness and love [of the Lord] will follow me [for the rest of my life]…" (vs. 6). As David reflected on the blessing and mercy of the Lord for his life, he only wished to be in the house of the Lord for the rest of his life.

It is not so important when this Psalm was written, but it comforted my heart in a time of learning to cope with my own psychological trauma. I used this Psalm for healing the symptoms of my PTSD. As a PTSD sufferer, I looked for healing grace from Psalm 23. It is important you know that it is not the psychology of healing PTSD. It is not a formula for healing symptoms of PTSD. It is simply my personal life experiences of learning to cope with my psychological trauma, based on meditation on this Psalm. It is a shift from psychological to spiritual battle. Part of my meditation was to examine my spiritual journey from brokenness to healing grace. As you read it, you might conclude that it was easy to meditate. In reality it was very difficult. It took me years to learn to overcome my psychological trauma.

In my personal meditation, I will share my psychological experiences of using the Scriptures and its imagery to heal my trauma. In my personal reflection, I will share about my Christian faith—how each verse from this Psalm impacts my life. By the end of each verse, I have written prayers to go along with my journey (and yours too).

I had been living with psychological trauma for many years after my family was killed. Nightmares, flashbacks, depression, anxieties, and fears filled my life. I did not know how to get rid of them. My personality was also shaped by these traumatic experiences. I never knew how to describe my personality or who I was back then. One thing I knew was that fear penetrated every area of my life.

Day and night, I was accosted by the flashbacks, and plagued by nightmares. Going to bed at night was living hell. I could hardly fall asleep, even though I was so tired from hard work. Physically, I was so exhausted, but my mind was constantly on red alert and filled with fear. There were so many enemies I could not see with my eyes. As soon as my head hit the pillow, my mind made me fear the Khmer Rouge soldiers (or anyone wearing a black uniform) could be chasing me. Usually, it would take me two to three hours to fall asleep. Sometimes within an hour or so the nightmares would return, and I could not get back to sleep. I had to stay awake until the morning or return to the psychological hell.

MY PERSONAL MEDITATION

Learning to surrender my life to my Shepherd

Every night, before I went to bed, I would spend at least thirty minutes or longer meditating on Psalm 23. I found a quiet place with no distraction or noise, where I could sit comfortably and relaxed. I took a deep breath and counted, "one, two, three." Then, I gently exhaled. I would recite in my mind, "Shepherd of my soul, please help me to surrender my life to You." I repeated, breathing deeply, until I felt totally relaxed. It was very helpful to learn to calm my mind though meditation.

Please note that the description of the nature of Psalm 23 is about the relationship between the shepherd and sheep. In this journey, I will address the Lord, God, or Jesus as "the Shepherd of my soul" throughout the whole book, except for direct quotes from the Scripture where I will maintain the original term.

Now, shifting from the psychological battle into my spiritual battle, I created imagery in my mind of a broken sheep in a deep, dark valley surrounded by foxes, wolves, and wild dogs. The fear was intensified. The sheep could not defend itself from the dangerous wild animals, but needed the protection of the shepherd.

Sheep are very vulnerable. They are defenseless. For example, dogs have their teeth and speed. Cats have their claws and speed. Horses have their speed, and they can kick and bite. Bears have their claws and teeth. Deer can run very fast. Compared to these, sheep have no defenses. They cannot even outrun any serious predator. Sheep have only one option—to totally depend on their shepherd. I envisioned myself as a broken sheep. I needed only the Shepherd of my soul to protect me. My Shepherd is my Defender, my Rock, my Deliverer, my Shield, and my Fortress.

Spiritually, it was a call to surrender my life to my Shepherd fully. I needed to give my life to Him and ask Him to protect me. In the midst of fear, I mostly needed my Shepherd to protect me and guide me through the deep, dark valleys.

Before I went to bed, I would imagine myself as a broken or vulnerable and weak sheep, vulnerable to all kinds of attacks from fierce animals. I could not defend myself. I just needed the Good Shepherd to protect me from being attacked by fierce animals. It was not easy for me to create imagery in my mind as a weak sheep. I could only see myself as a weak sheep surrounded by darkness, and in that darkness were my fears. Repeating "Be still and know that [the Shepherd is my] God" (Psalm 46:10) brought me a sense of security in the mighty hand of the Shepherd.

It was not easy for me to just sit down and meditate on the concept of being a weak sheep and on the Good Shepherd. When I was engulfed by darkness and fear, I just wanted to run and run, yet I did not know where to run to.

It was impossible to control my flashbacks—the more I tried to control them, the more they popped up in my mind. My heart started to race faster and faster. It was a long struggle for me to learn to be still. My mind was terrorized, and there was spiritual warfare in my mind. Sometimes, I felt as though I was being controlled by darkness.

As I imagined myself as a weak sheep running toward the Shepherd of my soul for protection, it gave me a sense of feeling secure, safe, and comfortable. The concept of relinquishing my fear to the Shepherd of my soul signified that I do not need to fight with my fear, because my Shepherd will fight for me. Without the Shepherd of my soul, I could never overcome my fears and depression. But I had to keep reminding myself to be still and know that the Shepherd of my soul would protect me. My Shepherd was my Rock of salvation. It took me years to meditate on this concept, and it helped me feel a sense of peace and serenity.

"The Lord is my shepherd, I lack nothing." This was a call to surrender my life to the Shepherd of my soul. I could not protect myself. I needed the Good Shepherd to protect me in the midst of my fears. Through my meditation I built the deepest security in the Good Shepherd of my soul. I felt secure in my Shepherd. He cared for my broken soul. When I meditated on the passage, "The Lord is the shepherd of my soul, I lack nothing," my broken soul felt secure.

PRAYER:

Lord, Shepherd of my soul, You are my Strength and my Defender. I am a weak sheep. I cannot protect myself from being disturbed by flashbacks and nightmares. I have no control over my mind. I need Your help. I need to surrender my mind to You to help me learn to overcome my flashbacks and nightmares. Only in You does my soul feel secure.

My Shepherd, I am weak. I cannot defend myself. I am helpless. My Shepherd is my Refuge, my Shield, and my Defender. I surrender my life to You. Help me overcome my flashbacks and nightmares. They make my life so miserable. I can no longer deal with them. Oh, Shepherd of my soul, I am a weak sheep. I realize that in my weakness I can never overcome my psychological trauma. I come to You, the Shepherd of my soul, to relinquish my mind over to You for protection. Shepherd of my soul, my mind can only find security in Your protection.

Shepherd of my soul, I surrender my fears, darkness, worries, anxiety, depression, flashbacks, and nightmares to You totally. My soul has been crushed, and only You can heal my broken spirit. I have been struggling to overcome my fears of flashbacks and nightmares for years. It has been so difficult to live with fear. Help me to be still and know that You are the Shepherd of my soul, and my Defender. Help my mind rest in Your serenity.

Shepherd of my soul, protect me from being disturbed by past painful experiences, and grant me Your peace and serenity. Shepherd of my soul, I call out to You to help me to feel secure in Your presence. Help me to be still and know that You are the Shepherd of my soul. Help me not to tremble with fear, but to be calm in Your presence. Shepherd of my soul, You are my Fortress. I call out to You in the midst of my fears and darkness. Deliver me from them, in the name of Jesus Christ, the Shepherd of my soul.

I would like to include a prayer from King David:

Teach me your way, LORD,
that I may rely on your faithfulness;
give me an undivided heart,
that I may fear your name.
I will praise you, Lord my God, with all my heart;
I will glorify your name forever.
For great is your love toward me;
you have delivered me from the depths,
from the realm of the dead.

(Psalm 86:11-13)

MY PERSONAL REFLECTION

*Patience is the art of learning to surrender
my heart to my Shepherd*

As I learned to meditate on the message, "The Lord is my Shepherd, I lack nothing" (vs. 1), it helped me a lot. It was a long, painful journey to learn to meditate on this concept, but it really helped me. Learning to surrender to the Shepherd never came easily and naturally. It took my strong personal determination to go the extra mile. As I examined my Christian faith, I realized that I needed to learn to relinquish my life to my Shepherd, and surrender to His will on a daily basis.

Living in this world of materialism, it is not easy to learn to surrender to the Shepherd of my soul. It is easier to fall into the trap of the pursuit of materialism. I have seen many Christians chasing their happiness through materialism and drifting away from worshipping their Lord. They failed to learn to relinquish their lives to their Shepherd. I had many good Christian friends who were more mature in their Christian faith than me, and they kept encouraging me to live by faith. They encouraged me to learn to surrender to the Lord. I often felt encouraged and honoured to get to know these good friends, and I highly respected them.

When I first went to the mission field, they laid their hands on me and prayed for me. Many years later, I met a couple of them again. I learned that their marriage was falling apart. They no longer remained faithful to the Lord. They drifted away, and lived their lives through drugs, alcohol, and other things.

There were many issues hindering my life and making it difficult to relinquish control to the Shepherd. There were times I questioned my Christian faith. I was not sure about my direction in life. I was not confident as to how long I could cling to my Shepherd. I was not yet convinced that my Shepherd would be with me forever. I was wrestling with learning to surrender.

Whenever I pondered my next steps, I always cried out to the Shepherd and asked for His direction. My Shepherd said, "Call on me in the day of trouble; I will deliver you, and you will honor me" (Psalm 50:15). In times of darkness and doubts, I called to my Shepherd to show me the way. In my desperation to get away from my restless nights, and the worry and anxiety, it could seem as though my Shepherd was out of reach. I wondered where my Shepherd was amidst my darkness. I wanted to see Him, to feel His presence, and to know He had heard my call. I tried to encourage myself that He was here with me. He was silent, and I needed to call to Him again and again.

It was so difficult for me in the middle of the night, to learn to be still and know that the Shepherd of my soul was my God. I could not be calm. I kept tossing and turning on my bed and wrestling with what was going on in my mind, waiting for the sun to rise so that I could get away from my thoughts. Most of the time after I woke up, I had to stay awake till the morning. No matter how hard I tried, I could not sleep.

Lack of sleep created many problems for my emotions, cognition, behaviour, and health. When I got up in the morning, I often felt confused and disoriented. I cried out, "Where is my Shepherd? Please lead me out of my confusion! Please help me to feel normal again!" I was not so sure about the meaning of life. I realized that my problems would not be resolved quickly and that there was no magical solution for me. I needed more time to learn to surrender to Him and do it all the time—in good times and bad.

I recalled an incident when I was flying from Taiwan to Toronto many years ago. Somewhere, halfway to Toronto, the airplane was hit by a strong storm. The airplane was suddenly in turbulence. My heart sank deeply. I was so scared. The pilot made an announcement about the storm, saying that the airplane could not avoid it. I wished I could get out of my seat and jump out of the airplane. But I had to stay still and fasten my seatbelt. There was nothing I could do.

Another incident was on the early morning of September 11, 2001. My wife and I were flying from Toronto to Edmonton to visit my foster mother. It was the first time I took my wife to meet my foster mother. We were so excited about the trip. The flight was very smooth. All the passengers in the plane were relaxed, reading books and newspapers.

Suddenly, the captain made a shocking announcement that the World Trade Center in New York was knocked down by terrorists, and the Canadian federal government had ordered all planes grounded immediately, to whichever airport was closest. Our plane was diverted to land at Winnipeg International Airport. The moment after the announcement was made, I could tell that everyone on the plane was praying. I doubt they were all Christians, but they all prayed for their safety. They all surrendered to the airplane. What else could they do but cry out to God for help? This is the way I needed to surrender my life to the Shepherd of my soul.

Once I was invited to share my own personal experiences on how to surrender to the Shepherd of my soul to a small group of believers. After I finished sharing, one young man asked me a good question, "Reaksa, when you totally surrender your life to the Lord, will you have any more problems? Will God protect you from all problems in life?"

It was a very good question. We assume that after we surrender our lives to the Shepherd, we will never have any more problems. I could not find any biblical references to support this wrong assumption. In fact, there is no guarantee in the Bible that, when you surrender your life to the Shepherd, you will never have any pain and suffering in your life. Jesus Himself demonstrated His pain and suffering on the Cross. When I think of the Cross, I often recognize in my heart that it is the trophy of pain and suffering I consciously need to carry until I personally meet the Shepherd of my soul.

Whenever I partake of the Communion service at church, I always remind myself that my Shepherd died on the Cross for my sin. I need to remind myself that there is no gift of being free from pain in this broken world. No matter what we are or who we are, we will eventually experience pain and suffering in our journey. There is no such thing as a normal life without suffering. Whenever I see the Cross, I never forget to remind myself that it is my trophy of suffering.

It is a good thing that our Shepherd offers a free invitation to us when we face pain in our journey: "Come to me, all you who are weary and burdened, and I will give you rest. Take my yoke upon you and learn from me, for I am gentle and humble in heart, and you will find rest for your souls. For my yoke is easy and my burden is light" (Matthew 11:28-30).

This is one of the invitations I need to learn to surrender to in times of trouble. My Shepherd's invitation is very simple. He is very gentle and humble. Being yoked with my Shepherd is about a relationship with Him— reading and meditating on His Word, praying to Him, and worshipping Him. I come to my Shepherd for His salvation. I received Him as the Shepherd of my soul. I realized that He would never promise to give me freedom from pain and suffering, but my relationship with Him enables me to face and go through all storms in my life. This means that I am united with Him, and I can learn to depend upon Him. His presence enables me to overcome my fears, anxiety, and depression. Life is a matter of learning how to surrender to the Shepherd of my soul—in good times or bad.

The more I learn about this surrender, the more I become aware that my journey is to depend on the amazing grace of my Shepherd. As I learn to surrender, He will guide me accordingly. I must learn to accept my Shepherd's yoke. He will take my heavy burden, and assure me of His presence with me. He will give me peaceful rest and guide me to overcome my heavy load. Learning to accept His yoke in the midst of heavy burdens is a big challenge. I want a quick response, and I want the heavy burden on my shoulder to be lightened sooner. As I learn to surrender, I entrust Him with my heavy burden, and rely on His teaching and guidance.

When I surrender, I learn to walk in fellowship with Him and I do not need to carry my yoke alone. He walks with me and helps me to carry my yoke. This is what I mean about the relationship with my Shepherd. While walking with Him, I learn that He enables me to carry my heavy burden with Him, no matter how difficult the situation I am facing. What is good about the Christian life is that it is not based on what I can do with my strength and wisdom, but on what my Shepherd does to transform me. He will eventually lead me to green pasture.

Learning to surrender to the Shepherd of my soul is a lifelong process. It is not one lesson, or one therapy session, or one preached message. It is a daily journey of my Shepherd's Word renewing my mind, body, and will, to learn to share my burden with Him. There is no quick road to spiritual maturity. I realize that learning to surrender my mind, body, and will to the Shepherd of my soul is a lifelong journey. Basically, it will take my personal self-discipline and consistency to work through the journey.

It does not mean that I say the prayer, "Shepherd of my soul, I surrender my mind to you. Please change me and make me a new person, free from all the problems," then get up the next day and become a faithful Christian. It does not work in this way. It takes my personal self-discipline and consistency, by the power of the Holy Spirit in me, to work through my thinking, learn to renew my mind, and change my behaviour. Spiritual maturity is a long journey and is often a painful process.

> *Therefore, my dear friends, as you have always obeyed— not only in my presence, but now much more in my absence—continue to work out your salvation with fear and trembling, for it is God who works in you to will and to act in order to fulfill his good purpose"* (Philippians 2:12-13).

Personal self-discipline is the inner motivation and determination to carry out my decision to follow my Shepherd in spite of inconvenience and hardship. When going through inconvenience and hardship, I keep reminding myself that I should never give up. I must carry on, yoked to my Shepherd. I keep reminding myself that I need to move forward with my Shepherd, and not allow my past painful experiences to divert me.

Consistency is my ability to do things repetitively without giving up. Patience is the art of learning to surrender my heart and soul to the Shepherd of my soul. The mind is the place of intellect, reason, and intentions. When I surrender my mind to the Shepherd, I can think about changing my heart and behaviour to conform to Him as He leads me. It may not be the way I want, but it is the way the Shepherd wants. For me, Paul has clearly stated how to renew our minds:

> *"Therefore, I urge you, brothers and sisters, in view of God's mercy, to offer your bodies as a living sacrifice, holy and pleasing to God—this is your true and proper worship. Do not conform to the pattern of this world, but be transformed by the renewing of your mind. Then you will be able to test and approve what God's will is— his good, pleasing, and perfect will"* (Romans 12:1-2).

In my early years as a new believer, I was impressed with this passage, *"Do not conform to the pattern of this world but be transformed by the renewing of your mind."* I think this is what the world needs to hear today. As a young Christian I wondered how I could avoid conforming to the pattern of this world. To put it simply, how could I live my life based on the Scripture? Or how could I live in such a way that would be acceptable to the Shepherd of my soul? In Canada if you just turn on your TV, you will see how the world tempts you with all kinds of materialism, covetousness, sexual sin, and immoral conduct. The pattern of this world calls us to worship sports stars, fancy cars, youth, beauty, big achievements, prestige, and money. This is how the world wants you to pursue happiness.

For me, it is interesting to observe that Paul says we must be transformed by the renewing of our minds. The mind is the key to the Christian faith. I must remind myself that, rather than continuing to conform to this world, I must be transformed by having my mind renewed by His Word. The Lord is my Shepherd, I lack nothing. In the Shepherd, I have everything. Nothing else is more important than having the Shepherd of my soul in my life. Nothing matters to me except longing to be led by Him.

Sophaly and I got married on November 11, 2000. We were blessed with many gifts (money and cups, pots, bowls, plates, photo frames, and so on). Among all the gifts, there was one special gift sent to us from Singapore. It was a card, blessing our wedding.

I opened the card: "Reaksa and Sophaly, I am so sorry for not being able to attend your wedding. I would like to share this Scripture with you: *'But seek first his kingdom and his righteousness, and all these things will be given to you as well'* (Matthew 6:33). When we got married, my parents passed this Scripture on to me. I would like to pass it on to you. We both learned to seek the Kingdom of God by surrendering to God first. It has been a blessed journey for us. May the Lord bless both of you. May you find happiness in the Kingdom of God."

This Scripture has been engraved in my heart since then. As I write this book, we have celebrated our twentieth anniversary and have been blessed with two wonderful children. I look back to the past twenty years as we have learned to surrender to the Shepherd of our souls together. We can see there was a combination of good times and bad, but it is worth the journey.

The art of seeking the Kingdom of God is to first surrender. In the Shepherd, I lack nothing and have tried my best to continue surrendering all these years. My needs will be met. In Him I lack nothing. My need for security will be met, as will my happiness. Through this journey with my wife, I have discovered the secret meaning of the Kingdom of God. It is stability, serenity, and contentment.

When I look at the life of Jesus, I can see that He first surrendered His life to the will of His heavenly Father, *"Very truly I tell you, the Son can do nothing by himself; he can do only what he sees his Father doing, because whatever the Father does the Son also does"* (John 5:19).

By the end of His ministry, He prayed, *"Father, if you are willing, take this cup from me; yet not my will, but yours be done"* (Luke 22:42). Jesus offered His life to His heavenly Father in obedience. He completely surrendered Himself to the will of His Father. As I look at the example of Jesus, there is a big spot inside my heart that is very uncomfortable. As a human being, it is not easy to reach such a level of surrender, but I must learn to surrender to the Shepherd of my soul, step by step. My ultimate purpose in life is to learn to surrender my life to Him.

PRAYER:

Lord, Shepherd of my soul, You are my Rock, and my Fortress. Please help me overcome my fears and depression. Help me learn to surrender my life to You totally. Help me learn to depend on Your will, not on my knowledge. Help me to come closer to You. Help me see Your will for my life. Help me walk in Your righteousness. Shepherd of my soul, I surrender all. I depend on Your grace. Please help me learn to examine my heart and guide me through the journey. Please help me learn to be still and know that You are the Shepherd of my soul. Please help me overcome my fears. Please help me learn to surrender to Your will. Amen.

I would like to include David's prayer for surrender to the Lord:

Trust in the Lord and do good;
dwell in the land and enjoy safe pasture.
Take delight in the Lord,
and he will give you the desires of your heart.
Commit your way to the Lord;
trust in him and he will do this:
He will make your righteous reward shine like the dawn,
your vindication like the noonday sun.
Be still before the Lord
and wait patiently for him;
do not fret when people succeed in their ways,
when they carry out their wicked schemes.

(Psalm 37:3-7)

YOUR REVIEW & REFLECTION

1. How do you learn to surrender your life to your Shepherd?

2. How do you get your mind transformed from the pattern of this world?

3. How do you seek the Kingdom of God in your life?

4. What do you want to see in your life from now on?

5. What hinders you from surrendering your life to your Shepherd?

6. Have you ever experienced trauma in your life? How have you coped with it?

7. What do you still need for peace and healing of these memories?

8. Can you relate to any of the symptoms described in this chapter (depression, sleep disorder, flashbacks, inability to concentrate, etc.)? Even if you may not have suffered as extremely as Reaksa has, God desires to bring healing to your particular struggle. What do you need to do to take the next step?

9. What do you want to pray for yourself?

2

My Shepherd Leads Me to the Green Pastures

A call to trust the Shepherd of my soul

"He makes me lie down in green pastures, he leads me beside quiet waters."

(Psalm 23:2)

As I contemplate this passage, I am reminded of when, as a young boy, I was uprooted from the city lifestyle and school and became a cowboy. In the Western concept, a cowboy is a man, typically one on horseback, who herds and tends cattle. In Cambodia, we went barefoot to tend the water buffalo and cows in the fields, which is a real challenge.

In the first few weeks, I did not know how to control the water buffalo and cows in the field. It took me a few weeks to understand their behaviour. Walking in the fields barefoot was miserable. I did not like the job at all, but I had no alternative. If I would not do the job, the village chief would not provide food for me. I worked for one day and got two meals.

However, after a few months of tending the cows and water buffalo I began to enjoy it. I really enjoyed seeing the greenery and the river every day. The beauty of the countryside was peaceful and serene. During hot days, my friends and I would go down to the river and swim for a few hours. We played on the mudslide. We would play buffalo fighting in the mud. Once we were tired, we would get out of the river to sit down under a big tree and watch over the water buffalo and cows grazing in the fields.

There were about four hundred water buffalo and cows. Our job was to bring them to where there were green pastures and water resources. Water buffalo would never survive without water. They would graze along the river or lake, then wade in the water for a little while, and then get out of the water to graze again. If the day was really hot, they would stay in the water for a long time.

Cows are different, as they do not like to stay in the water. They would graze along the river or lake. When they were thirsty, they would go to the river to drink and come back to graze. If the day was hot, they would find shade under the trees and rest for a little while, then go back to graze again.

I observed that wherever there were a lot of good green pastures, the cows and water buffalo would stay in the same field to graze till late afternoon, and then we would bring them back to the village. However, if the fields did not have enough green pastures, they kept moving from place to place and gave us a hard time controlling them.

As cowboys, we always gave them the best green pastures and water resources. Otherwise, we would have a hard time taking care of them. I learned that among the cows, there were one or two troublemakers who would often lead the others in a different direction. We made sure the troublemakers did not go out of our sight, because they could lead the others far away, making it difficult to bring them back to the village in the evening.

As I examined this verse, I recalled that King David himself was a shepherd and knew where to lead his sheep to the place filled with green pastures and quiet water. In his old age, he realized how the Lord had likewise led him into a sweet and beautiful place with green pastures and quiet water. It is a place filled with peace and serenity.

I think that in modern life we often lack access to the peace and serenity of nature. In malls, commercial buildings, city parks, and other urban public spaces, all we can find are fountains and "greenery." If you visit Singapore, you will see many public fountains. Even at the airport there are water fountains or green gardens inside the buildings. It looks nice, and some are beyond our imagination, but it does not reflect real nature. It reflects modern technology.

When I visited some of the fantastic places in Singapore, I took the time to enjoy some sights of "man-made nature." But it did not last long. After spending a few hours enjoying these man-made natural spots, I came to realize they did not provide peace and serenity because they did not reflect genuine nature.

In the Eastern concept, a shepherd is responsible for leading his sheep into green pastures. Not only will the sheep find plenty of grass and water there, but they will also be safe. The description in Psalm 23:2 reflects genuine nature, peace, and serenity. David imagined himself as a sheep being led by the Shepherd to green pastures and quiet waters. It is a call to trust in the caring and loving heart of the Shepherd. I can imagine seeing green fields extending along a valley, with a small stream running quietly, the sound of birds chirping, and fish swimming in the stream. The scenery is filled with the spectacular natural beauty of nature, the smell of fresh grass, and a gentle breeze.

David wrote this verse in which he contemplated himself as a sheep being led into beautiful scenery, where the sheep felt secure under the mighty hand of the Shepherd of the soul. The sheep could move around in the field freely without fearing other animals that might be fierce. The sheep calmly trusted the Shepherd.

My Personal Meditation

The Shepherd of my soul leads me to feel peace and serenity

I have learned that relaxation is very helpful for meditation. I recite, "Shepherd of my soul, please lead me to feel peace and serenity." I take a deep breath in and out, reciting this phrase again and again. It was hard to spend ten to fifteen minutes reciting the same words again and again, but it helped me to calm my mind. It also helped me to concentrate on my Shepherd. As I recite this phrase, I envision myself seeing beautiful scenery with green pasture. It helps my mind to calm down and relax. Relaxation is the most effective way to calm my mind, and it also helps me to meditate on the Scripture. If I could not relax, my mind would be flying everywhere.

I indicated that the first verse of Psalm 23 is a call to surrender to the Shepherd of the soul. This second verse, for me, is a call to trust in His mighty hand. It is a genuine relationship between the shepherd and sheep. For me, meditation is the power of discipline of the mind. I tried to picture myself as a sheep in the green field. As I meditated on this second verse, I began to question—how could I trust the Shepherd in the midst of my flashbacks, nightmares, depression, fears, emotional imbalance, and so on? This Scripture indicates a genuine relationship of a sheep trusting the shepherd.

I once sat down with my friend James. He had a lot of experience raising sheep in England and New Zealand. He had about one hundred sheep. He told me that he knew most of his sheep, and his sheep also knew him. He knew a few troublemaker sheep in the flock and the weak sheep as well. If the troublemaker sheep attempted to lead the flock in a different direction, he would yell to the sheep, and they would change their direction or stop moving. He even named some of the sheep. He knew all his sheep and his sheep knew his voice.

He said, "Reaksa, you know that when I started raising the sheep, I had no idea how to raise them. It was hard for me when I first started, but after a few years I really enjoyed raising them. They knew my voice. When I called them by name, they came to me. It took time to develop a trusting relationship with them." I was fascinated to hear this. He said that he could sit down with me for a few months and teach me things about raising sheep.

As I listened to him, I reflected on when Jesus said, "I am the good shepherd; I know my sheep and my sheep know me" (John 10:14). And Jesus also said, "My sheep listen to my voice; I know them, and they follow me" (John 10:27). I think it would take time to build up a trusting relationship between the sheep and the shepherd. I would like to hear the voice of my Shepherd.

Picturing myself as a sheep, I trusted the Shepherd of my soul to make me lie down in green pastures. There was no better way for me as a weak sheep than to look to the Shepherd of my soul to bring me to meet my desire of green pastures and quiet waters. However, in reality my life was full of emotional crises and psychological trauma. How could I bring myself, as a broken sheep, to trust in the Shepherd of my soul for healing?

Before I share my personal journey, let me point out that emotional and psychological damage can take only a few seconds to turn a person's world upside down. But it takes many years to get them healed and set free!

Some people make a desperate attempt to come out of the emotional and psychological damage to start a new, wholesome journey. Many other people can never get out of the pit of emotional and psychological damage. They often find themselves engulfed by negative thoughts and feelings, which rob them of simple normal activities and enjoyment, and drive them down to deep, dark depression and anxiety. In the worst cases they drown themselves with alcohol and drugs, with predictable consequences. Some take their despair with them to the grave. I know I once thought I was unrepairable.

I meditated on this passage and imagined myself as a broken sheep. Although my trusted Shepherd led me to this green pasture, my heart was still turbulent. The hurt and pain inside me created a sense of restlessness and helplessness. I tried my best to shut down all the internal conflicts, but it was useless. It was impossible to gain victory over the psychological trauma in my mind by suppressing it.

Now, I've learned to trust the Shepherd of my soul to lead me to the green pastures.

How did I eliminate the unwanted memories in my mind while seeing myself in this place of peaceful solitude? As I tried to meditate on the concept of peaceful solitude—green pastures and quiet waters flowing down a stream—my soul felt secure in the mighty hand of this great Shepherd. It had been a very long struggle for me to try to overcome my nightmares, flashbacks, and emotional disturbances. I had to learn to trust Him from the bottom of my heart—trust that this Shepherd would lead me step by step to a place of peaceful solitude, restoring my life in every way.

My meditation was very difficult. I was wrestling with my mind. It was so hard for me to see the green pastures and hear the quiet waters running in the creek. The enemies in my mind made it impossible to see the beauty of the green pastures. My ears could not hear the stream, no matter how hard I tried. I could only hear the hacking blades and the screaming of my family and other victims.

Closing my eyes to meditate on this passage and learning to trust the Shepherd was very challenging for me. I tried so many times, but it was impossible to control my mind. Eventually I realized that it was not only a psychological battle, but also a spiritual one. My mind was controlled by the spirit of darkness. As soon as I tried to meditate, I would feel the fear of darkness consuming my life.

There was a shadow of darkness pulling me or holding me in a dark cave. In my struggle, I realized that I needed to take time to pray to cast out the spirit of darkness from my mind. I prayed to my Shepherd to set me free from the dark cave. "Shepherd of my soul, I take refuge in you; You are my Protector. I ask You to cast out the spirit of darkness from me. Set me free from the bondage of darkness." I recall a few times, I stopped meditating and got up to shout loudly, "In the mighty name of Jesus, the Shepherd of my soul, I cast out the spirit of darkness from me."

I never gave up trying to meditate on this verse. I placed all my psychological disturbances on the Shepherd of my soul, who led me to see the beauty of the green pastures in my mind. I desperately needed my mind to rest and be at peace so I could sleep.

As a sheep I needed to trust the Shepherd of my soul to lead me. I cried out to my Shepherd and told Him my need,

When I am afraid I put my trust in you.
In [the Shepherd], whose word I praise—
in [the Shepherd] I trust and am not afraid.
What can mere mortals do to me?

(Psalm 56:3-4)

As I concentrated on these verses, I came to realize that it was impossible to find peace after meditating only a few times. Although traumatic memories would disturb my mind, I kept asking my Shepherd to help me to be still so that I could feel peace. Learning to pray to this Shepherd only one or two times would never help me get rid of my emotional disturbances. Developing a habit of meditating on these Scriptures was to increase my trust in the Shepherd to lead me to peace and serenity.

I felt that peaceful sleep would never come naturally to me, but at least I was learning to increase my trust in the

Shepherd of my soul. Sometimes, when wrestling to sleep, I recited these verses, "*In peace I will lie down and sleep, for you alone, Lord make me dwell in safety*" (Psalm 4:8). "*Lord, how many are my foes! How many rise up against me! Many are saying of me, 'God will not deliver him.' But you, Lord, are a shield around me, my glory, the One who lifts my head high. I call out to the Lord, and he answers me from his holy mountain. I lie down and sleep; I wake again, because the Lord sustains me. I will not fear though tens of thousands assail me on every side*" (Psalm 3:1-6).

After years of prayer and meditation, I felt as though the Shepherd of my soul granted me a peaceful moment amidst my struggle in life. I learned to rest my soul on my Shepherd. I strongly believe that my Shepherd will continue to care for my soul. In my prayer below, I hand all my emotional and psychological disturbances to the Shepherd of the soul and let Him lead me to peace:

PRAYER:

Lord, Shepherd of my soul, You are my Deliverer and my Salvation. I desperately need Your guidance to lead me to the green pastures. I long to see the beauty of the green pastures You will lead me to see. I trust that You will lead me to feel peace and serenity. I have faith that You will heal my trauma.

I yearn for the sound of quiet waters. Shepherd of my soul, I desperately need You to help me overcome my fears. Help me to feel peace while I go to sleep. Help me trust You more and more so that I can feel secure while I am sleeping. Shepherd of my soul, deliver me from all nightmares, flashbacks, and fears in the night whilst sleeping.

Shepherd of my soul, please protect me from being disturbed by nightmares, flashbacks, and fears during the night when I sleep.

Shepherd of my soul, You are my Protector and Defender. Please guide my soul into a place of serenity. I pray all of these in Your name. Amen.

I would like to include King David's prayer:

Be merciful to me, LORD, for I am in distress;
my eyes grow weak with sorrow,
my soul and body with grief.
My life is consumed by anguish
and my years by groaning;
my strength fails because of my affliction,
and my bones grow weak.
Because of all my enemies,
I am the utter contempt of my neighbors
and an object of dread to my closest friends—
those who see me on the street flee from me.
I am forgotten as though I were dead;
I have become like broken pottery.
For I hear many whispering,
"Terror on every side!"
They conspire against me
and plot to take my life.
But I trust in you, Lord;
I say, "You are my God."
My times are in your hands;
deliver me from the hands of my enemies,
from those who pursue me.
Let your face shine on your servant;
save me in your unfailing love.

Let me not be put to shame, Lord,
for I have cried out to you;
but let the wicked be put to shame
and be silent in the realm of the dead.
Let their lying lips be silenced,
for with pride and contempt
they speak arrogantly against the righteous.

(Psalm 31:9-18)

MY PERSONAL REFLECTION

Learning to be still and know that the Lord
is the Shepherd of my soul

In my childhood I had tons of experiences fishing with my brothers and father. We went fishing for survival. We caught big fish and small fish. We took them all home.

But fishing in Canada is different from fishing in Cambodia. A few years after I settled in Canada, my friends took me fishing with them. After that first time, I was addicted to fishing. In Canada, there are certain rules and regulations we have to obey. Fishing is a lot of fun and very relaxing, particularly because I really like nature. I like to see the beauty of nature as the sun rises and sets. Most of all, I like to hear the gentle sound of a stream, and I like to see the water running downstream. Whenever I go fishing, I feel relaxed.

After a fishing trip, I noticed I could relax and sleep better. Catching fish was not my ultimate goal, but if I could catch some, it was a big bonus. My passion for

115

fishing was about relaxing in nature. It helped me learn how to relax and be patient. It helped me learn to be still and listen to the voice of my Shepherd.

When fishing, I learned to recite my prayer inside my heart: "My Shepherd leads my soul to the quiet water. Help my soul to feel peace inside me. Shepherd of my soul, please help me and heal my broken soul. My Healer, please help me to overcome my flashbacks and fears." I had discovered that reciting my prayers while fishing helped me to feel relaxed. It also helped me to feel a sense of peace. My mind was not occupied by anxieties or fears. I find that a fishing trip is a time of tranquility. Most of all, fishing is fun and relaxing. My mental focus on nature helped me to relax and I noticed that I did not see flashbacks attacking me. It was perhaps that my mental focus on nature helped reduce my flashbacks. Or perhaps that my mind was in touch with nature and allowed me to speak to the Shepherd of my soul freely.

I realized that fishing was my best activity for learning to be patient and still. I am a type-A person. It is not easy to remain patient and stay still while fishing. I had to learn stillness and calmness. With my temperament, my friends did not believe that a type-A personality like me could find solitude while fishing. I could not explain to them the reason I could calm myself and stay still while fishing. I just told them that when I sat down in front of my books and computer, my mind went crazy, like popcorn popping; flashbacks, especially, attacked me, in and out. I could not control my mind at all. I could not concentrate on my studies.

But when I sat down with my fishing rod looking at the stream of water, my mind was so relaxed and calm. As my mind was in touch with nature, I could stay still and relax. I could hear the stream running without being disturbed by flashbacks or fears. I could feel peace and serenity. It was just a different way of mental adjustment. I often recited my prayer, "Be still and know that the Lord is my Good Shepherd." I took a deep breath, "Be still and know that," releasing my breath out, "He is my Good Shepherd." None of my friends believed what I told them.

I said to them, "I would like to take early retirement, and would like to organize fishing trips for those who suffer from PTSD to go fishing with me, and I will guide them to learn how to be still." Sometimes when the fish bit, it distracted my prayer, but I still found my fishing trips helped me to relax and build up my trust in my Shepherd. I know He wants me to stay connected with Him.

Many good friends often thought that I was "the lunatic fisherman." I must admit that I was a little crazy about fishing, but I learned that my fishing trips helped me to overcome my flashbacks during the day. The flashbacks stopped attacking me. Wherever I go, I look for an opportunity to go fishing. I have travelled to Australia, the USA, many places in Canada, Thailand, and the UK, and I often managed to go fishing.

Once I was invited by my friend Dick to speak at a private school and a few other places in Atlanta, Georgia. One day there was no speaking engagement for me, and he asked me if I was interested in going to see the national museum. I told him honestly that I had no desire to go and visit the museum, but if I could go fishing for a few hours I would be happy. Dick was so surprised, but as a polite host he managed to get a fishing license for me and took me to a place where I could fish while he read a book. I got a few fish and released them back into the water and was happy.

Another time I was invited to speak at the Apologetics Conference in British Columbia by Andy Steiger, the conference organizer. I told him that I did not want to fly all the way to BC to speak for only a few hours. We left it at that. He mentioned my name to Henry, a friend of mine who attended church with Andy. Henry told Andy, "If you really want Reaksa to come and speak, you need to tell him that you can take him fishing." Andy wrote me back and offered me the bonus of going fishing, so I made the trip to speak at the Apologetics Conference. It might sound a bit crazy, but it is true to my personality.

Whenever I went to BC, I would try to get together with Tim, a pilot from Abbotsford, to go fishing. We didn't care much about getting fish, but we could spend four to five hours standing by the stream fishing and talking about our theology, our faith, and more. We still call each other and talk about going fishing together. Our friendship bonds over fishing, relaxing, talking about theology, and laughter.

In Cambodia, after I returned there from living in Canada, I had my own private fishing ponds. No matter how busy I was, I could still manage to go fishing in my ponds and recite my prayers to my Shepherd. I just wanted to go fishing and relax at my fish ponds. It also helped me to cope with the daily stress of my ministry.

Many years later, I came to realize that in order to develop a trusting relationship with my Shepherd, I needed to be open to Him seeing deeply into my inner brokenness. I needed to honestly acknowledge my own weakness to heal, and I needed to bring my pain and brokenness to my Shepherd. A genuine trusting relationship requires honesty. I needed to tell my Shepherd how broken I was and how crippling my inner fears were to me. I desperately needed a healing grace so that I could function normally in my daily life. I knew that my Shepherd listened to my prayers.

The moment after I was baptized, as I emerged from the water, I vowed that I would never give up my faith and trust in my Shepherd. No matter what happened I would remain faithful and trust Him for the rest of my life. In my journey of learning this trust, I met many good Christian brothers and sisters who told me many good things about their lives.

As I tried to understand their perspectives, I came to realize they often asked God to help them succeed or give them some kind of guarantee of prosperity as a basis for their trust. I was once like them too. I could recall my prayers when I was in the refugee camp in Thailand. I was in deep, dark depression after I was rejected by the United States Immigration and Naturalization Service. Knowing I was not allowed to resettle in the US, I gave up hope for the future and found the greatest enemy of my life: hopelessness.

One evening, out of desperation, I left my house in the camp. Alone, I decided to kneel down and pray, "Lord God, if you take me to Canada to start a new life again, I will put my trust in You and I will give You my life." Many years after I became a Christian, I realized that it was not a good prayer to test the Shepherd of my soul. It was not faith in my Shepherd. I did that because I was so desperate for something better in my hopelessness. I just wanted to get out of the refugee camp.

After I became a Christian, I went to study at Tyndale University and Providence Theological Seminary for six years. Being a new Christian, I was not sure what it meant for me to trust the Shepherd. Many good friends at school tried to encourage me and said, "When you trust, He will lead you to a better life." Others told me that when you trusted your Shepherd, He would provide for your needs and more.

How did I learn to trust? Once I heard a pastor preaching about trusting in the Shepherd. He said, "Sometimes God tells you to do something that appears foolish and illogical—for example, Jesus telling Peter to walk on the water toward him, or Abraham being told to bring his son for a sacrifice. Another example is God telling Gideon to bring only 300 Israelites to fight against 135,000 enemy soldiers—the odds were 1 to 450. In human logic these are impossible odds. It sounded foolish, but Gideon obeyed God and the Israelites won the battle. To trust God is to have faith in Him. Faith is obeying God when you do not clearly understand what God is asking you to do." As I heard these words of encouragement, they inched me along in my struggle to capture the real meaning of trusting the Shepherd of my soul.

When I established the church in Siem Reap a few friends came to visit. After we had breakfast one morning, before they returned home to Thailand, one sister asked for my permission to speak to me. She opened her Bible and said, "The Lord told me to share this message with you from Proverbs 3:5-6, *'Trust in the LORD with all your heart and lean not on your own understanding; in all your ways submit to him, and He will make your paths straight.'"*

After she finished reading these two verses to me, she said, "Brother Reaksa, in your journey you will face disappointment, hurt, and discouragement, but you need to trust the Lord and learn to depend on Him. Do not depend on your own understanding. He will guide you through your journey. My prayer for you is that you will learn to trust the Lord and learn to depend on Him in all you do."

I was so grateful to hear such words of encouragement. It was an assurance for me to learn to trust Him "in all my ways." Part of her encouragement had touched my heart too. Sometimes I was too arrogant and proud of my knowledge, my education, and my achievements. In good times or bad, life is a matter of learning to trust this Shepherd by relying on His all-sufficient grace and not on my own attributes.

David trusted his Shepherd who loved and cared for him, so he experienced peaceful solitude. In the midst of distress, depression, hopelessness, loneliness, the loss of a loved one, betrayal, financial difficulty, disappointment, rejection, failure, family hostility, and pain, nothing else is more important than trusting in the love of the Shepherd of the soul, regardless of what may happen to us next. David not only surrendered his life to the Shepherd, he also had the courage to be led by Him until he arrived in green pastures. David trusted his Shepherd wholeheartedly.

After years of emotional and psychological distress, I came to realize that I desperately needed this kind of peaceful life—a life of trusting the loving care of the Shepherd. It had been more than twenty years since my family was taken away, but I could not make myself trust anyone. I used to tell a few very good friends that I could not trust anyone and I could never trust myself. They asked me the reasons. I did not know how to explain it to them, but I said, "Well, if you were in my shoes and your world was turned upside down, and if you had gone through terrible trauma, then you would know why I can never bring myself to trust anyone or even to trust myself."

I realized that response was my defense mechanism to avoid facing the reality of hurt in my heart. The truth was that my psychological trauma deeply wounded my deepest sense of self. I personally lost an essential part of myself, including the ability to trust myself.

The deep wound inside me led me into personal isolation. I could never forget that, as a young boy, my family was snatched from me so suddenly and so cruelly! I was left in the jungle alone for a few days with no one to protect me. I was not sure how I survived. I was grieving by myself near the grave of my family for three days. I was utterly alone and lost.

The terror of rejection pierced my heart. The distress I felt became an obstacle in learning to trust the Shepherd of my soul. It took me many years to realize this sense of brokenness, this sense of a spirit shattered. My personal studies of psychology helped me to realize this terror of rejection had robbed me of any trusting relationships. I knew that the terror of rejection inside me needed to be healed by the Shepherd of my soul. Only consistent prayers to Him could restore my ability to trust.

I became really fascinated with the concept of David picturing himself as a sheep being led to the green pastures and quiet waters. It is a beautiful picture.

As I reflected on this passage, I was gripped by the essential meaning of trust in the Shepherd of my soul. I needed to learn to hear the voice of my Shepherd. The Shepherd wanted me to totally trust Him and to experience the fullness of life in the green pastures that He has for me. When I became a Christian, I was not good at being led by my Shepherd. I did not know His voice. But as I learned to build my relationship with Him, I started to recognize His voice and know where He was leading me. It took me many years to learn to recognize and listen to His voice.

Once I was invited to speak at a private Christian high school in Singapore to about 3000 students. After I finished, one of the teachers came to talk to me privately. She said that she used to go to church and was actively involved in all church activities, but she had so many problems in her life, including health problems, financial crises, and family hostilities. She felt rejected by her church members and her family. She could see no hope.

Through tears she told me, "I wanted to feel peace. I want Him to lead me to some kind of peace and security. But my mind is so disrupted. I am so depressed. I cannot bring my mind to see the green pastures." She wanted to hear something from me. I was speechless. I was not sure how to encourage her after I heard all the problems in her life.

As I listened to her painful story, I realized that she had allowed her trust in the Lord to drift away just when she needed Him the most. In her confusion and struggle she failed to remain faithful to the Lord. In fact, I have seen many Christian friends who have failed to remain faithful to the Lord when their lives were hit by many adversities and difficulties. How do you trust God when your life is filled with countless problems?

In my twenty years of ministry in Cambodia, I went through countless adversities. My brother-in-law was killed by robbers on the road at night. I had to drive to pick up his body and bring it home in the middle of the night. It was so hard for me to see my only living sister suffering such a tragedy in the family. Many extended family members were angry at me for not providing some financial support for my sister's family. Others accused me of betraying my traditional Buddhist culture. They did not want to see me introducing our Christian faith into their society.

About six years later, one of my church leaders in the countryside died in this tragic accident. His son-in-law went down the well to clean it. Because of the lack of oxygen deep in the well, he collapsed. The church leader went down to try to rescue his son-in law and suffocated as well. Both died in this tragic accident. The whole church fell apart and no one wanted to attend the church again.

Many people in the village were so angry at me because I had planted a church in their village. They blamed me for bringing the Western curse into the village and believed that the village spirits were angry and had killed the church leader. A few elders and a village chief came to me and begged me to stop planting the church. I was so discouraged. I felt attacked from many different directions. Most believers drifted away from the church because of the tragedy.

A few years after that, I was hit by another storm. A young lady, a new mother and a church member, had a seizure and a stroke. She was in a coma, so her family sent her to the emergency hospital in Thailand. I went to see her in the hospital and spoke to her doctor. He told me that her prognosis was very grim. There was little chance that she would survive. I was shocked and helpless. I knelt down with her husband and prayed for her. We cried until we had no more tears. We asked God for His mercy for this young mother.

I wrote emails to many friends to ask for financial support to help pay for the medical bills. I was able to raise more than enough money to cover her medical bills. I gave all the money I raised to her. In the end, she recovered from her coma. While she was in bed, many friends went to visit her. She was talking about buying a new smartphone, a small car, a new plot of land, and so on. It created a lot of jealousy in the church. I was in big trouble. Many church members started spraying bullets at me; words of gossip were flying all over the church. I was accused of favouritism. I was accused of stealing money and so on. I could account for all the funds, as I kept all receipts and documentation.

A few church leaders in Singapore who supported my family came to visit me, talked to me, and looked at the documentation and its transparency. After further investigation, no wrongdoing was found. I knew that my integrity was questioned. One of these leaders is my good friend and he had no question about my integrity, but it was unpleasant to face this kind of accusation. I felt tremendously pressured. I was deeply shocked at how my best intentions and kind actions could be so misinterpreted. I was so discouraged to the point of brokenness. Even worse was for me to see my wife, who had sleeplessly looked after the baby girl for almost a month while her mother was in the hospital in Thailand. She was very disappointed and hurt. I was in a state of deep, dark depression. I could not sleep for a few weeks. All I received back from my actions of kindness was ingratitude. My reputation was destroyed. How could I learn to accept this kind of adversity? One of my friends came to me and asked me a good question, "Can you forgive her?" I did not respond to him, but I asked, "What would you do if you were in my shoes?"

When facing life's adversities, I count it a privilege to learn to stand firmly on my Christian faith. Facing adversities is when I need to trust my Shepherd the most. James said, *"Consider it pure joy, my brothers and sisters, whenever you face trials of many kinds, because you know that the testing of your faith produces perseverance. Let perseverance finish its work so that you may be mature and complete, not lacking anything"* (James 1:2-4).

I have learned many lessons about pain, including letting the pain inside me be transformed with my Shepherd's help. I regard these lessons as a way the Shepherd purifies my heart. These lessons have taught me to trust my Shepherd to heal my pain and lead me to green pastures, and not to lean on my own understanding during difficult times. I would take one more step closer to the Shepherd of my soul, admit the hurt and pain, and claim my liberty to remain strong in my faith. I honestly count these trials as a way of purifying my faith.

How can I remain faithful to the Shepherd of my soul in a time of trial? It is a journey of learning to depend on the Shepherd daily. It is a conscious choice I make every day. Every morning when I get up, I remind myself that I trust the Shepherd of my soul and I will depend on His grace. Trusting is an ingredient of faith and hope. When facing hardship, I try my best to live to my full potential as a Christian. I live in hope for the courage to move on by relying on the grace of my Shepherd. Paul had many things to say about the grace of God for those who are suffering:

I consider that our present sufferings are not worth comparing with the glory that will be revealed in us. For the creation waits in eager expectation for the children of God to be revealed. For the creation was subjected to frustration, not by its own choice, but by the will of the one who subjected it, in hope that the creation itself will be liberated from its bondage to decay and brought into the freedom and glory of the children of God.

We know that the whole creation has been groaning as in the pains of childbirth right up to the present time. Not only so, but we ourselves, who have the firstfruits of the Spirit, groan inwardly as we wait eagerly for our adoption to sonship, the redemption of our bodies. For in this hope we were saved. But hope that is seen is no hope at all. Who hopes for what they already have? But if we hope for what we do not yet have, we wait for it patiently.

In the same way, the Spirit helps us in our weakness. We do not know what we ought to pray for, but the Spirit himself intercedes for us through wordless groans. And he who searches our hearts knows the mind of the Spirit because the Spirit intercedes for God's people in accordance with the will of God.

And we know that in all things God works for the good of those who love him, who have been called according to his purpose. For those God foreknew he also predestined to be conformed to the image of his Son, that he might be the firstborn among many brothers and sisters. And those he predestined, he also called; those he called, he also justified; those he justified, he also glorified.

What, then, shall we say in response to these things? If God is for us, who can be against us? He who did not spare his own Son, but gave him up for us all—how will he not also, along with him, graciously give us all things? Who will bring any charge against those whom God has chosen? It is God who justifies. Who then is the one who condemns? No one. Christ Jesus who died— more than that, who was raised to life—is at the right hand of God and is also interceding for us. Who shall separate us from the love of Christ? Shall trouble or hardship or persecution or famine or nakedness or danger or sword? As it is written: "For your sake, we face death all day long; we are considered as sheep to be slaughtered." No, in all these things we are more than conquerors through him who loved us. For I am convinced that neither death nor life, neither angels nor demons, neither the present nor the future, nor any powers, neither height nor depth, nor anything else in all creation, will be able to separate us from the love of God that is in Christ Jesus our Lord (Romans 8:18-39).

This is a full picture of the grace of God that Paul refers to when suffering. It is a full account of comfort in time of suffering. I have read this passage so many times. The first few times I read it, I could not picture the grace of God. It did not make any sense at all. I could not capture the beauty of the grace of my Shepherd. Over many years, I read it again and again until I did receive comfort from this passage.

The grace of the Shepherd of my soul came to me when I reached rock bottom. I cried out to the Shepherd to release me from my suffering and lead me to peace. When

I was weakest, I cried out to be delivered from my misery. I could tell that there was strength pushing me from behind. Then the grace of the Shepherd came to me and I felt His comfort. It took years beyond my suffering to fully realize the power and beauty of the grace of my Shepherd.

I had faith that my Shepherd would never toss me out of His love, and I had hope that He would lead me to peaceful solitude. To trust in my Shepherd was to focus my eyes on Him even as the storms of my life tossed me about. My eyes would never lose sight of Him. It was not easy to consider all kinds of adversities and difficulties in life as pure joy, but the process of purification helped me to see the genuine meaning of His faithfulness. My suffering taught me the precious lesson that I need to depend on my Shepherd to move on in life.

As mentioned previously, David tasted all kinds of adversity in his life, but he unwaveringly trusted his Lord. He cried to his Lord to deliver him from his enemies.

Be merciful to me, my God,
for my enemies are in hot pursuit;
all day long they press their attack.
My adversaries pursue me all day long;
in their pride many are attacking me.
When I am afraid, I put my trust in you.
In God, whose word I praise—
in God I trust and am not afraid.
What can mere mortals do to me?

(Psalm 56:1-4)

David trusted the Lord and prayed to be delivered from his enemies.

Vindicate me, Lord, for I have led a blameless life;
I have trusted in the Lord and have not faltered.

(Psalm 26:1)

David trusted the Lord his whole life. He never faltered in his trust in the Lord even though he faced various difficulties in his life.

My journey in life was not as smooth as I expected. However, I always tried to maintain my faith on the road of righteousness, and I hoped that my Shepherd would lead me to green pastures. I can now see a glimpse of green pastures in front of me. I will strive to trust my Shepherd for the rest of my life. I need to stay close to Him all the time.

Jesus said,

"Remain in me, as I also remain in you.
No branch can bear fruit by itself;
it must remain in the vine.
Neither can you bear fruit unless you remain in me."

(John 15:4)

In my journey to move on to green pastures and quiet waters, nothing is more important than trusting in the unfailing love of the Good Shepherd.

But I am like an olive tree flourishing in the house of God;
I trust in God's unfailing love for ever and ever.

(Psalm 52:8)

No matter what strikes my life, I need to persevere in my trust in the mercy of my Shepherd for the rest of my life. David said,

Blessed is the one who trusts in the LORD,
who does not look to the proud,
to those who turn aside to false gods.

(Psalm 40:4)

PRAYER:

Lord, Shepherd of my soul, You are my Strength and my Rock. Please help me remain faithful to You. Help me to trust You from the bottom of my heart, so that I will always obey You. Help me to be humble. Help me to rely on You, the Shepherd of my soul. Whatever the circumstance of my life, please help me to trust You and rely on Your all-sufficient grace. Shepherd of my soul, help me overcome my terror of rejection so that I can trust You fully. Restore my health and help me to trust You in times of difficulty. Amen.

David prays:

You have searched me, LORD,
and you know me.
You know when I sit and when I rise;
you perceive my thoughts from afar.
You discern my going out and my lying down;
you are familiar with all my ways.
Before a word is on my tongue
you, Lord, know it completely.
You hem me in behind and before,
and you lay your hand upon me.
Such knowledge is too wonderful for me,
too lofty for me to attain.

(Psalm 139:1-6)

Your Review & Reflection

1. Do you know where your Shepherd is leading you?

2. Are you willing to follow your Shepherd fully?

3. Have you learned to listen to the voice of your Shepherd?

4. What helps you trust your Shepherd?

5. When you have to deal with fear or anxiety, or when depression attacks you, how do you deal with it?

6. What imagery stands out for you in Psalm 23 that helps you most in your struggles?

7. What part of Reaksa's story speaks most powerfully to you in your healing journey?

8. Write down your prayers:

3

MY SHEPHERD RESTORES MY SOUL

*A call to walk forward with the
Shepherd of my soul*

As I mentioned before, I have no experience raising sheep and I have never been a shepherd, though I used to be a cowboy in Cambodia, guiding water buffalo and cows. But sheep are different. My friend told me, "Sheep are dumb and directionless and defenseless. If left in the wild, they would never survive."

I also asked my friend, "How did you guide your sheep?"

He said, "It depends on the behaviour of the sheep. Typically, it can be in front, beside, or behind the sheep." It is interesting to learn how the shepherd guides the sheep.

David acknowledges how the Shepherd restored his soul and guided him through his journey, "He refreshes my soul. He guides me along the right paths for his name's sake" (Psalm 23:3). There are treasures to mine in this verse.

Let's look at other versions of Psalm 23:3: "He restores my soul" (ESV). "He renews my strength" (NLT). The word "restore" means "bring back" or "to reinstate." "Renew" means "resume after an interruption." "Refresh" means "to give new strength or energy to reinvigorate." I think that from a linguistic point of view these words contain a different meaning, but personally and based on my journey, I prefer to use the word "restore."

In this short verse, it is hard to get a full picture of what David actually intended to say. Perhaps he was backsliding from his Lord, or perhaps he was exhausted from working too hard or running away from his enemies. In the modern world, we could say that David is running out of gas.

Speaking from the perspective of the shepherd's care and sheep's need, we can understand that the shepherd may think that the heat is extreme, the sheep are tired, and he wants to bring the sheep to drink and rest in the shade. In another case, a sheep was lost and the shepherd found her and brought her back to the flock. Spiritually, David might have realized that he had committed a sin against God when he stole Bathsheba to be his wife. He prayed to the Lord to restore him back.

MY PERSONAL MEDITATION

The Shepherd of my soul restored my life

To meditate on this verse, I recited this phrase in my mind, "Shepherd of my soul, please restore my soul." I took a deep breath, and released it. I recited this verse again and again.

I can imagine David in his old age, sitting in his palace, reflecting on his life, and composing Psalm 23 to acknowledge that the Shepherd restored his soul and led him into righteousness. As he looked back over his life, he may have realized that during part of his journey he wandered from the Lord or sinned against his God (possibly after he was confronted by Nathan in 2 Samuel 12). Not only did his Shepherd lead him to green pastures and quiet waters, but He also restored him back onto a path of righteousness.

Because of his experience as a shepherd boy, David would have been aware of the nature of the sheep and that they could easily get lost in the valley. A few of the sheep David was once responsible for might have got lost in the valley, and he would have spent time bringing them back to the flock. David did imagine himself as a lost sheep until the Shepherd restored him and led him onto a righteous path.

I am reminded of what David wanted in his life:

One thing I ask from the LORD, this only do I seek:
that I may dwell in the house of the Lord
all the days of my life,
to gaze on the beauty of the Lord
and to seek him in his temple.
For in the day of trouble he will keep me safe in his dwelling;
he will hide me in the shelter of his sacred tent
and set me high upon a rock.

(Psalm 27:4-5)

David is very committed to staying in the house of the Lord. It is a safe place where he can depend on his Shepherd. David longs to worship his Shepherd for the rest of his life and is happy in the house of his Shepherd.

David knows he is being led on paths of righteousness, trust, and holiness. For David, the priorities of worshipping and honouring the Lord for the rest of his life became more important than anything else.

As I meditated on this passage I imagined myself as a lost sheep away from my Shepherd. I created a picture in my mind of me searching for my Shepherd. I just wanted to be with my Shepherd. My psychological trauma had given me more than enough troubles in my life. I had fought so hard to control my mental restlessness and gained little ground. Now, as a broken sheep coming to my Shepherd, I wanted to rest in His mighty arms and allow Him to take charge of my mental restlessness, my fears, my depression, and my nightmares.

As I prepare to meditate on my surrender to the Lord, I invite the Shepherd to take charge of my mind. I invite Him to take my fears, nightmares, flashbacks, and depression away. I come to my Shepherd for restoration of my brokenness. The need to feel normal in my life. I do not want to be terrorized by flashbacks and depression. I continually trust that only the Shepherd of my soul will heal my psychological trauma. In Him, my mind can be peacefully restored by His amazing grace.

When I felt fully embraced by the Healer of the soul and the Rock of my soul, I allowed myself to be healed. I felt release and relaxation. I felt safe and secure in the arms of my Good Shepherd. In my struggle to calm down my psychological restlessness and depression, I fell into the mighty arms of my Shepherd with my brokenness. Psychologists or psychiatrists could never help me to feel safe and secure—only the Healer of the soul could give security for my broken soul.

Learning to surrender my life to the Lord was hard at first. Then, as I learned to trust the Lord in times of difficulty, it became easier as time went on. Placing my mind in the mighty hand of the Good Shepherd was beginning to feel natural.

PRAYER:

Lord, Shepherd of my soul, You are my Saviour and my Deliverer. I am grateful that you spared my life from the grave. My Shepherd, my mind is crushed and my spirit is in despair. My normal night's sleep is restless. I cannot cope with my nightmares, flashbacks, and anxiety. I have no peace in my life. My health has deteriorated. My emotions are unstable. Please restore my health. I cannot think properly. My mind is being disturbed by my fears, nightmares, and flashbacks. My life is full of confusion and restlessness. I cannot function properly. My normal thinking becomes disrupted by the symptoms of PTSD. Shepherd of my soul, please restore my health. Please help me to have the joy of a simple life. Create in me a clean heart and help me to move on, day by day, by relying on your amazing grace. Amen.

David said this prayer after he was confronted by Nathan. He realized that he had sinned against God. I also prayed for restoration from the Lord:

Have mercy on me, O God,
according to your unfailing love;
according to your great compassion
blot out my transgressions.
Wash away all my iniquity and cleanse me from my sin.
For I know my transgressions,

and my sin is always before me.
Against you, you only, have I sinned
and done what is evil in your sight;
so you are right in your verdict and justified when you judge.
Surely I was sinful at birth,
sinful from the time my mother conceived me.
Yet you desired faithfulness even in the womb;
you taught me wisdom in that secret place.
Cleanse me with hyssop, and I will be clean;
wash me, and I will be whiter than snow.
Let me hear joy and gladness;
let the bones you have crushed rejoice.
Hide your face from my sins and blot out all my iniquity.
Create in me a pure heart, O God,
and renew a steadfast spirit within me.
Do not cast me from your presence
or take your Holy Spirit from me.
Restore to me the joy of your salvation
and grant me a willing spirit, to sustain me.

(Psalm 51:1-12)

MY PERSONAL REFLECTION

The grace of my Shepherd was sufficient for me

When I was young, I used to use two oxen to pull a cart or to plow the field. After I used them in the morning, I would release them to graze in the field. When the temperature was very high, I would take them to the water and give them a shower; basically I just poured water on them. Then I would take them to rest in the shade. There I would provide them grass to eat before I worked them again when the heat subsided. I worked them and I fed them. I took care of them. The genuine relationship between me and the oxen was gradually built over time.

When in the shade, I would gently pat their heads, talking to them, showing my appreciation for how they helped to pull the cart. With my own ability and strength, I could never pull the cart for more than one metre. No way; it was impossible. The two oxen would lick me. I hugged them as well. I could tell they appreciated how I took care of them by feeding them and putting them in the shade. I refreshed them and renewed their energy. I know that oxen's needs and sheep's needs may not be the same, but the concept of caring for both oxen and sheep may be quite similar.

As I look back over the past forty years of my life, I can see countless blessings and mercies of the Shepherd in my life, and how the Shepherd of my soul has restored me to where I am now. The moment I went down to the grave, I felt that I was done forever. There was no way, from a human perspective, I could have survived the Killing

Fields. If I were to have a million dreams, I could never dream that I would still be alive after it was all over.

This was the deepest and darkest moment in my life. The chance that I would survive from the grave was one in a million. That was my perspective when I was in the grave, lying amongst the dead bodies. I could not see a glimpse of survival from the Killing Fields. While lying there, I cried out to the spirits of my dead family to take me with them. I did not want to live. It was too much pain for me as a young boy to bear. I just wanted to die. After I escaped from the grave, I sat down on a poisonous snake in the jungle. I actually said to that poisonous snake, "Bite me and take my life." I lost my desire to live. I wandered in the jungle, a boy with no family, no home or village to return to if I were to avoid recapture. I was a shell of a person, dead inside except for incredible pain. Death seemed to be the only way for me to ease my pain.

Hindsight tells me that at that time, I wore my darkest glasses. I could see only the dark side of life. My darkest glasses were filled with bitterness, disappointment, hurt, hatred, and revenge. I could not see a glimpse of light for my life. I considered that I was lucky to have survived the Killing Fields. I thought that I was a tough boy. I could handle all my pain. I could handle my life in my own way. The truth was that I was living my life with bitterness and depression.

Many years later, I learned that the darkest glasses I wore for so many years kept me from seeing a better future. I could see only my bitterness. Later, this bitterness robbed me of seeing a blessing from the Shepherd in my life. My view was coloured by darkness—it shaped my way of thinking and behaving. Later, this darkness developed into the attitude of my heart. I could not see the positive view of my future my Shepherd was showing me. Most of all, the dark glasses I wore robbed me of joy in life. I could not see the blessing of my life. I had no hope. I could not even see the blessings my Shepherd had for me. The impact of psychological trauma caused me to see only darkness in my life. I could never see anything better for me.

Now that I have been wearing my glasses of the grace of my Shepherd, I can see the beauty of life. I can see how my Shepherd has restored my soul step by step since the time of my darkness—when I was in the grave. Even though it was a long, painful journey, I can see the hand of the Shepherd on my life. It took me many years to see how He has restored my soul. I was lost, but now I have been found and restored by my Shepherd.

It is a joy to see the grace of my Shepherd for restoration. He lifted me from the grave of the Killing Fields. He led me through the jungle filled with landmines. He was with me in the refugee camp for five years. He opened the door for me to the land of opportunity in Toronto, where I restarted my life. He embraced me like a lost sheep. I became one of His flock. He sent me to schools for more than ten years to learn how to shepherd others. Eventually, my Shepherd sent me back to my country for twenty years, to tell others the message of His love and forgiveness. What restoration! I am a living testimony of the all-sufficient grace He extends. His grace is more than enough for my life. What a wonderful Shepherd I have!

In the time of my loneliness, the Shepherd of my soul connected me with a friend named Phil Ulrich. He was a student at Tyndale University. He was a very young, handsome man. He often spoke very loud. I met him and got to know him like my brother. Once he and his room-mate, Andrew, took me to the ravine behind the school. When we got there, Phil and Andrew started to yell as loud as they could. I was so stunned. I did not know what to say to them. They were laughing and laughing. It was a typical way of young Canadian students.

Even though sometimes he gave me a hard time by teasing me, he loved and cared for me. His mother, Carolyn Ulrich, became like a foster mother to me. She loved me like her own son. I have loved her like my own mother. She took an interest in me and encouraged me to love the Lord. Even though she lived far away from me, she always called me and told me not to work too hard and to take time to relax. She quoted a popular Canadian saying, "All work and no play makes Jack a dull boy." When I finished my master's degree, she came across the country for my graduation. I was so happy to have a mom at my graduation. It made me feel like a little part of my family had been restored to my life.

Rudy and Sharon Dirks' family is also fulfilling the substitute part of my family. After I got to know them at school, they took me into their family. It was a special priv-ilege to have them be like my family. They totally accepted me without question. They have loved me uncondition-ally. In my heart, I knew that they loved me like their brother. In Canadian culture, there are three important occasions: Easter Sunday, Canadian Thanksgiving, and Christmas. I never missed joining this family for these spe-cial occasions.

After they went to serve the Lord as missionaries in Botswana, they introduced me to their parents from both sides. I got to know them and they accepted me into their families. Sharon's parents loved me like their son. They accepted a total stranger like me into their family. I loved Sharon's father, Art, like my honourary father. I highly respected him. I got to know him personally. He often encouraged me to love the Lord—seeking first the kingdom of God. He also taught me the value of the Mennonite Christian faith. I am not a Mennonite Christian, but my Christian faith has been rooted in their values. This family has richly blessed me with an abundant Mennonite legacy and spiritual values. I felt honoured to be adopted into their family.

When I was single, I came for Christmas celebrations with this Mennonite family, and there was always an extra chair for me. After I got married to my wife, Sophaly, there were two extra chairs for my family. After Philos and Sophia were born, there were always four extra chairs for us. In good times and bad, I honestly shared with them. They embraced me and my family. They have walked with us and they still count us as part of their family. I respect Rudy like my big brother. My kids would address Rudy and Sharon as Uncle and Auntie.

When Art, his twin brother (who I called Uncle Fred), and I were together, we collapsed into peals of laughter. We had a lot of things in common. For one, we are all die-hard Maple Leafs fans. We talked a lot about hockey.

On Christmas 2017, I called from Cambodia to say Merry Christmas to Art. I found out that he was in the departure lounge on his way to meet his heavenly Father. He told me that he was ready to meet Him. Before he hung up his phone, he blessed me with his prayer. Five days after that, he was promoted to be with his heavenly Father. I had planned to return to Canada for his funeral, but I took the wrong passport and missed my flight. I grieved for a few months.

When I went back to Canada to visit my Mennonite family in Niagara-on-the-Lake, I first went to put flowers on Art's grave. I just wanted to show my respect to my honourary father. It was a blessing for me to be surrounded by good people. I am forever grateful to the Shepherd of my soul for sending these beautiful people into my life. In times of my depression and darkness, they took me under their wings. They loved me unconditionally and lifted me up in those times. They encouraged me to look to the Shepherd of my soul for help. Often I was ready to give up. I could not bear the pain of depression, but they came to my life to give me a hug and pray for me. Their care and love encouraged me to keep moving on. I am forever grateful to my Shepherd for guiding me to know them. Words cannot express my gratitude for what they have done for me.

The most blessed restoration of my life was having my own family. Years after I lost mine, I longed to have my own family. I wanted to recreate a real sense of family. My foster mother often encouraged me to settle down. I just told her that I would leave my life to the Shepherd of my soul to prepare the way. In school, during a course on marriage and family, I learned one phrase, "If you marry a good wife, you will be twice blessed, but if you marry the wrong one, you will become a philosopher." I like to study philosophy, but I never wanted to become a philosopher. This phrase got stuck in my mind for years. I was so afraid to settle down. The statistics of the divorce rate in Canada were very high. It prompted me to think a lot about married life. I did not want to become a philosopher. Period.

When I arrived back in Cambodia in May 1999, I met Dr. Andrew Kwong, the former dean of Phnom Penh Bible School. He asked me, "Reaksa, would you like to marry a local girl?" I quickly responded, "I do not see that happening." He asked me, "Why not?"

I did not know how to answer him. At that time, I was not ready to settle down. In my heart, I knew that I longed to have my own family to replace the one that I had lost many years ago. In some respects, I personally felt pulled by the two cultures—Canadian and Cambodian. I was born and raised in the Cambodian culture, but I had been living in Canada for more than ten years. My thinking and behaviour had been shaped by the Canadian culture. I forgot my own roots. I needed to learn to acculturate myself into the Cambodian culture. When I first went back to Cambodia, I had a hard time re-adjusting to the Cambodian culture and I found myself judging it. Instead of learning to accept it, I became so defensive that it took me some time to learn to observe and accept my original culture. With all of this going on in my head, how could I agree to marry a Cambodian woman? I was wrestling with the two cultures. In fact, I was stuck between them.

About six months after I returned to Cambodia, a friend from Toronto came to look for a wife in Cambodia. His relatives introduced him to many girls in the city. One of the girls was Sophaly. My friend went to visit Sophaly a few times, but his mother who lived in the other province did not want him to marry a city girl. She wanted my friend to marry her relative instead. Then I went to tell Sophaly that my friend decided to follow his mother's wish, which meant that he would not come back to her.

Later, I took Sophaly for a date. I was not interested in pursuing a relationship with her because she was not a Christian. I shared with her about the salvation of Jesus Christ and also invited her to come to church. I introduced her to a local church pastored by my friend Bunthan. He helped Sophaly to understand the meaning of salvation in Jesus Christ. She became interested in knowing more about Jesus and started to attend church regularly. A few months later, she accepted Jesus Christ as her personal Lord and Saviour.

After that, I dated her regularly. Her mother knew she had been dating me and that I was a Christian, and she strongly objected to our relationship. She heard a lot of fabricated bad stories about Christians, so she did not like the idea of her daughter dating one. She heard that when someone became a Christian, he or she had to disown his or her family and could not burn incense sticks for the ancestors anymore.

One afternoon while I was lecturing at the Bible School, I got a surprise phone call from Sophaly's mother. She called me and told me, essentially, to get lost. Imagine my disappointment. I told Sophaly not to worry about her mother's objection. "All you need to do is pray to the Lord. If the Lord prepares our lives together, He will pave the way for us." I could tell that she could not yet understand my perspective. I then returned to Canada in early 2000. About six months after that, her mother went to visit her friend who is a Christian, and heard of the salvation through Jesus Christ. It was the first time she heard the true story of Christian people. Finally, she approved our relationship. I returned to Cambodia to lecture on counselling and psychology at the Bible School again in

October 2000. On November 11, 2000, I got married to Sophaly. I am blessed to have this wonderful woman in my life. She was not raised in a Christian family. She had no knowledge of being a missionary, but she demonstrated a heart of submission and was willing to stay with me in the mission field for twenty years after we got married. She loves me unconditionally. She is a pleasure to be around. I admire and appreciate her trustworthiness.

The Shepherd of my soul has blessed us with two wonderful children—Philos and Sophia. When I was doing my undergraduate study, I loved to study philosophy. The word "philosophy" means the love of wisdom. I promised myself that if I had children—a boy and a girl—I would name the boy Philos and the girl Sophia. Philos means "love;" Sophia means "wisdom." The two together mean philosophy—the love of wisdom. My dream has been fulfilled. I am forever grateful to the Shepherd of my soul for giving me a family. I feel so happy to have a family of my own. From the moment they were born, I never grew tired of loving them. It took me twenty-five years after my family was taken away to have my own family. It was good to have my foster mother and Rudy and Sharon as a substitute family, but to have my own family, I feel genuinely blessed by my Shepherd. I am blessed with a wonderful family. It has been a great joy raising my two wonderful children in a Christian home. Whenever I was at home, I would never forget to spend time reading the Bible with them. In fact, I started reading the Bible to them as soon as they were born. I built up a habit of reading it to them every night. It has been a fantastic journey with my kids. In fact, reading the Bible and praying at night before going to bed became a traditional habit for my family.

My son, Philos Reaksa Himm, was baptized by Pastor Timothy Phau at Mount Horeb Presbyterian Church in Singapore on June 2, 2019 at age sixteen. Here is what Philos shared as his testimony after he was baptized:

"Hello, my name is Philos Reaksa Himm. I am here today by the grace of God, and I want to speak a bit on why I want to be baptized. I feel honoured to be baptized by Pastor Tim. I'm glad that he's not having a stroke this time. I was born in Canada, but my parents took me to Cambodia when I was a baby. When I was around four, my parents took me back to Canada. Since I was small, I was raised in a Christian family and was told about the many stories in the Bible with pictorial Bible stories. The first book I got to read was not a school textbook, but the Bible stories.

"At home my Father made an agenda for my family that in the morning we need to read a devotion, and at night we read the Bible and pray together as a family. We rarely miss reading the Bible, unless my father is away, but most of the time he would call us and tell us to read the Bible. So, reading the Bible has become a habit in my life. Most of the time I don't understand all the things in the Bible, but I keep reading. Until now, I have finished reading the Bible twice. However, the most important story to me was the story of Jesus' salvation and how He came into the world more than 2000 years ago to die on the cross for our sins. The famous verse John 3:16 says, `For God so loved the world that He gave His one and only Son, that whoever believes in Him shall not perish but have eternal life.' I want to be baptized because I want to enter the family of God. I will become a child of God.

"I admit I am a sinner and I need Jesus as my Lord and Saviour. 'If you declare with your mouth, "Jesus is Lord," and believe in your heart that God raised him from the dead, you will be saved' (Romans 10:9). Now being a child of God, I need to stay connected with Jesus. Meaning I need to build a habit of reading His Word daily, praying, participating in Bible studies, and worshipping. On the 24th of June, my family and I will return to Canada to start a new life. We will face hardships with acculturation. Please continue to pray for us, especially for me as I will have to meet new friends, and continue to learn to walk in His righteousness. Once again thank you so much, Pastor Tim."

Up to the time of this writing, Sophia is not yet ready to be baptized. We have been praying for her to be ready for baptism.

How did the Shepherd lead me all these thirty years after I became His sheep? In addition to restoring my family, the Shepherd of my soul has also gradually restored my mental health. After spending many years meditating on Psalm 23, I could see the joy in my life. My depression has subsided. I have a positive outlook. My nightmares and flashbacks no longer trouble me. It is the greatest miracle of my life. Nightmares were the most destructive to my health. By the grace of my Shepherd, I have been healed from my nightmares. As of now, they do not attack me. I can think better. I can see joy in my life when I get up in the morning. I never imagined I could be healthy again after many years of living with nightmares and depression. *"He heals the brokenhearted and binds up their wounds"* (Psalm 147:3).

The second part of Psalm 23:3 is: *"He guides me along the right paths for his name's sake."* In Eastern cultures, the shepherd may have the responsibility of guiding their sheep. Sometimes only a narrow path runs between the pasture and these fields where crops are growing. The sheep are forbidden to eat in these fields. The shepherd's responsibility is to guide sheep along such a path, not allowing any to get into the forbidden area, or he may be asked to pay damages to the owner of the crops.

As a cowboy, I learned many skills on how to guide the water buffalo and cows. Paddy rice farming in Cambodia is never fenced because the fields would be too big to fence. Near the village, the pathway for the water buffalo and cows to walk is very narrow. In the rice farming season, if we were careless and allowed them to eat the paddy rice, we would be punished by the village chief. He would not allow us to eat dinner as a punishment. Our responsibility was to prevent them from eating paddy rice. We had to carefully guide them from the village to the fields in the morning, and from the fields back to the village in the evening, not allowing them to go off the narrow path. Water buffalo and cows were easily tempted to eat the green paddy rice on the farms.

Human beings easily get lost in the pattern of this world—the way we live in the modern world. We tend to conform to the pattern of this world rather than be transformed by the knowledge of Jesus Christ. In the last twenty years, I have travelled to speak at many churches in more than ten countries around the world. I met many people and church leaders in those countries. I heard countless stories from former church leaders and former believers who got lost in the pattern of this world of materialism.

Many of my church members who drifted away from the Lord stopped coming to church, and went on to pursue materialism and happiness in the secular world. I have learned that most of them tried to pursue a better lifestyle, such as having a big house, a good car to drive, and a good job. But they have lost their focus on the Cross and lost their first love (Revelation 3). Eventually, they drifted away from the Lord. Some of these church members got involved with alcohol, drugs, and gambling. Their lifestyle became destructive to their children. I grieved over these church members.

In the summer of 2004, I was invited to speak at a church in South Carolina. My friend Alvin introduced me to three former US marines who had served in Vietnam. I sat down and listened to their conversations about how they were sent to fight in Vietnam and how they suffered from PTSD. They were talking about their nightmares, flashbacks, depression, other psychological disturbances, and so on. I learned that they all could not cope with their psychological trauma and could not handle their marriages. In fact, all of them were divorced from their spouses. I asked them what caused their divorces. They told me honestly that they were drinking too much and they also used cocaine. Instead of learning to cope with their emotional and psychological trauma, they turned to alcohol and drugs as their coping mechanisms.

As I listened to them, I could identify with them too. I remembered when I was a policeman. In the evening when I could not sleep, I had to have a few drinks to knock myself out so I could sleep. I could hardly fall asleep unless I knocked myself out with alcohol. Later, I did not like alcohol. It gave me a lot of trouble, so I decided to stop drinking it. Getting drunk was an easy way to deal with an instant psychological disturbance, but it would create more problems. Alcohol and drugs seemed to be the most

153

powerful substances to make them forget their emotional and psychological trauma. It made them feel good.

When I became a Christian, sometimes, when I could not sleep or the nightmares woke me up in the middle of the night, I was tempted to drink alcohol to help me sleep again. Several times in the middle of the night, after wrestling on the bed for many hours, I was so desperately tempted to have a drink, but I was grateful I never fell into that trap. The Shepherd of my soul led me to meet many good people, who encouraged me to remain faithful, and they prayed for me. However, I also met a few bad friends too. They tried to introduce me to drugs to make me feel better and help me to get a good sleep.

They would say, "Try one smoke. You will forget everything."

Out of desperation to get a good sleep, I was tempted to take it, but morally I was very strong to resist such an offer. I am grateful to the Shepherd of my soul that He never allowed me to be hooked on drugs, and I stopped hanging out with these friends. I was aware of the consequence of such drugs. I would never allow myself to be misled by my bad friends.

Do not be misled: "Bad company corrupts good character" (1 Corinthians 15:33).

I am grateful to the Shepherd of my soul for guiding me to meet all the good people who have helped me to fix my eyes on the Shepherd and, also, directed me onto the righteous path. Without their love and guidance, I might have been lost in this world. This world is full of temptation. It is so easy to fall into the trap of the temptation.

These good people have helped me to walk on His righteous path. My Shepherd has brought me to safe pasture as well. I recall when I escaped from Cambodia with a group of people, we walked through the jungle for two days and two nights. Before reaching the refugee camp along the Thai-Cambodian border, we encountered a group of bandits or thieves. They shot at us. All the refugees were scattered in the jungle. Everyone ran for their lives. I was trained in the police force; running in the morning was a daily habit of mine. I got lost by myself in the deep, dark jungle. While running, I saw a lot of dead bodies. I just kept running and running until finally I was out of the jungle. I was so frightened. I did not know what was wrong with the dead bodies, but I just kept running and running.

After running for more than an hour, I was so thirsty. There was no water to drink. I saw three men who were bicycle taxi drivers (they were trying to transport people from the jungle to the refugee camp for a fee). I could see from a far distance that they were not armed. They were ordinary people. I tried my best to run toward them. I could see that they were trying to lift their hands up to signal me not to run. I did not understand what they were trying to signal to me; I just sprang toward them. When I reached them, I could hardly catch my breath. I realized they were shocked to see me running in the jungle. One of the men asked me, "Where were you running from, and why did you run by yourself in the jungle?" I did not answer him quickly. I tried to catch my breath.

Then I told them that I was running for more than an hour in the jungle by myself. There were some refugees who were attacked by a group of bandits or thieves. I got lost by myself. Another man said, "It is impossible. You know, you were running through landmines—a million pieces of landmines in the ground. No one has ever come out of that jungle alive." As soon as I heard what he told me, I almost died of a heart attack. I felt frozen. I knew that he was not joking with me. I had seen a lot of dead bodies in the jungle. At that time, I thought that I was lucky. As I examined, through the perspective of Psalm 23:3, *"He guides me along the right paths for his name's sake,"* I could see the mighty hand of my Shepherd was on me. He protected me from stepping on the landmines. If the Shepherd of my soul, my Protector, had not been guiding my every step as I moved through the jungle, I would have been blasted off by a landmine. Every time I came through this particular verse, I could only picture the Good Shepherd in my life. I am forever grateful to Him.

PRAYER:

Lord, Shepherd of my soul, You are my Protector, my Deliverer, and my Provider. I thank You so much for taking me from a long journey of brokenness to Your healing grace. Many years ago, I never imagined I could reach this stage of healing. Now, I can see the joy in my life. Shepherd of my soul, I feel restored by Your abundant grace. I am grateful that You have guided me to meet many good people who have shown me love and care despite my brokenness. Thank You for bringing them into my life. Thank You for bringing my health back. Now, I feel I can think normally again. My nightmares, flash-backs, and depression have subsided from my life. Thank You for restoring my family. I am blessed to have a family of my own. My family has brought me a lot of great joy in my life. Thank you, the Shepherd of my soul, for leading me to meet many good people who helped me to walk through the journey of darkness toward peace and serenity. I thank You for guiding me through the land-mines. It was impossible to make my journey through the jungle without Your protection. I am grateful to my Shepherd that I am able to smile again. Amen.

I would like to conclude with King David's prayer:

Create in me a pure heart, O God,
and renew a steadfast spirit within me.
Do not cast me from your presence
or take your Holy Spirit from me.
Restore to me the joy of your salvation
and grant me a willing spirit, to sustain me.

(Psalm 51:10-12)

Teach me your way, Lord,
that I may rely on your faithfulness;
give me an undivided heart,
that I may fear your name.
I will praise you, Lord my God,
with all my heart;
I will glorify your name forever.
For great is your love toward me;
you have delivered me from the depths,
from the realm of the dead.

(Psalm 86:11-13)

YOUR REVIEW & REFLECTION

1. Have you ever sinned against your Shepherd? If so, write down your sins:

2. What do you want your Shepherd to restore you to be and to do?

3. How do you want to build your relationship with your Shepherd?

4. How do you want your Shepherd to guide you for the next ten years?

5. How do you prevent yourself from being misled?

6. Have you ever been spiritually lost? How do you find your way back to the Lord?

7. What spiritual practices do you find most helpful for you to experience God's restoration in your life (meditation, contemplative silence, prayer, sharing with others, communal worship)?

8. Write down your prayers:

4

My Shepherd Walks Me Through the Darkest Valley

*A call to walk with the courage
to overcome fears*

Verse four of Psalm 23 is a very interesting description in which David describes his circumstance as very dangerous. *"Even though I walk through the darkest valley, I will fear no evil, for you are with me; your rod and your staff, they comfort me."* David describes his circumstance as, "walking through the dark valley of the shadow of death." He was not afraid of the dark valley nor death. During David's journey from a shepherd boy to a king, he knew what it meant to walk through the shadow of the valley of death. In one circumstance in his life, he tried to escape from King Saul. This is the full picture of how he pictured the deep, dark valley of his life.

As a shepherd boy, he stood bravely against the giant Goliath. He was just a young boy who had no experience in the military. His older brothers, who were professional soldiers in the armies of Israel, opposed his going to fight against Goliath. Logically, from the human perspective, they figured that their shepherd boy was going to walk to the valley of death; he was surely going to die. It was impossible to fight this giant of a man of the Philistines. All the armies of Israel could not face him. There was no way young David could come back alive and unharmed! He was done for as soon as he got to the valley. No one in Israel was brave enough to stand up to fight against the giant Goliath. But David had the courage to stand up to fight him.

> *David said to the Philistine, "You come against me with sword and spear and javelin, but I come against you in the name of the LORD Almighty, the God of the armies of Israel, whom you have defied. This day the LORD will deliver you into my hands, and I'll strike you down and cut off your head. This very day I will give the carcasses of the Philistine army to the birds and the wild animals, and the whole world will know that there is a God in Israel. All those gathered here will know that it is not by sword or spear that the Lord saves; for the battle is the LORD's, and he will give all of you into our hands."* (1 Samuel 17:45-47.)

David actually won the battle against the giant Goliath. The armies of Israel chased all the Philistines away. Before David became the King of Israel, he went through a lot of valleys of death in his life. King Saul chased after him from one valley to another to kill him. After King Saul died, David became the King of Israel. He still had many enemies, even within his own circle, plus the Philistine armies. He truly knew the shadow of death in his life, and he wasn't just speaking of the experiences of others walking in the midst of dangers—a deep, dark

162

valley of the shadow of death. The dangers in his life were real, and he would never escape from the deep, dark valley of the shadow of death. The shadow of death engulfed his life, but he feared no evil. He never allowed himself to be crippled by fear. He knew that the Lord would protect him from all enemies.

I find this verse so encouraging, and it is full of meaning for my personal journey of learning to overcome my fears. The shadow of death in my life after the terrible experience of the Killing Fields were the fears and depression that crippled my life for years. I did not have the courage to face the fears inside me. When fears took deep root inside me, I became absolutely paralyzed and I could not stand up for myself. I could not face others. For me, this verse is a call to walk with the courage to overcome fear. Courage is not the absence of fear, but the presence of the Good Shepherd of the soul with me. My Shepherd was my Protector and Defender.

As I looked back to those years of my darkness, I came to realize that I was trying to fight my internal fears by my own strategy and in my own way. The more I tried to fight with my own strength, the more I sank deeper and deeper into despair and hopelessness. I could not control my fears. When I studied this passage, again and again, I realized that the Shepherd of my soul wanted me to stop fighting by myself. I needed to trust my Shepherd, and learn to walk with Him. He would defend me. In the valley of my life, my Shepherd wanted me to learn to walk with Him. He wanted me to have the courage to walk with Him. He was my Defender. He would guide me through the deep, dark valley of my life and I should not be afraid. For years, I tried my best to run from the deep, dark valley of my life—the psychological problems in my life—but it could never make my life better. In fact, it made my life more miserable.

The Shepherd of my soul wanted me to learn to walk with Him in the deep, dark valley of my life, and allow Him to protect me. He wanted me to face the enemies inside me, and walk with Him, and keep trusting Him to set me free from all my fears. The journey of my life was to learn to surrender my life to the Shepherd of my soul, to trust Him, to be restored by Him, and now to walk with courage to overcome my fears with this precious Shepherd of my soul.

MY PERSONAL MEDITATION

My Shepherd helped me to walk through
the valley of the shadow of death

Finding a quiet place to sit down and concentrate on this verse is very important for me. The best way to start meditation is to sit down and relax, take a deep breath again and again, and recite these words in my mind, "Shepherd of my soul, my Defender, my soul Protector, please help me to walk through the deep, dark valley of my life, and help me to overcome my fears." It took me some time to learn to build up my habit of meditating on the Word of my Shepherd.

> *Even though I walk through the darkest valley,*
> *I will fear no evil, for you are with me;*
> *your rod and your staff, they comfort me.*

(Psalm 23:4)

This verse describes the most important relationship between the shepherd and the sheep. The shepherd's responsibility was to escort his sheep through the deep, dark valley where they might be in danger of being attacked by wild animals. The shepherd would need to protect his sheep and comfort them in times of danger. The shepherd would use his rod and his staff to protect his sheep in the deep, dark valley. If the sheep was lost in the deep, dark valley, the shepherd would need to go to look for the sheep and bring her back to the flock.

I personally found this verse to be the most important part of my meditation, but it was not easy for me to sit down to meditate on this verse. Many years after my family was killed, I was living in shock and fear, and was psychologically crippled. Now, sitting down and closing my eyes, and painting a picture of myself sitting in the deep, dark valley of death, I was filled with terrible fear. The fear of darkness haunted my mind constantly. I was reminded of the first night after my family was killed. I was just a young, helpless little boy, sitting by myself in the deep, dark jungle. "I was lost in the deep, dark jungle; I cried out for someone to help me to get out of the jungle. No one came to rescue me." This traumatic event was glued in my mind for years.

As I tried so hard to imagine seeing myself as a broken sheep in the deep, dark valley with the Shepherd of my soul, I could hardly paint the picture of myself in the dark valley. My mind was constantly disrupted by my fears—I could not concentrate on my meditation. There was no sense of peace and serenity in the deep, dark valley. It was too real for me. As soon as I sat down to meditate on this part, I could hardly be still. The fear inside me made my mind restless.

Just pretending to sit down and be still, knowing the Shepherd of my soul was with me in a different setting, not in the deep, dark valley, was not so difficult to imagine. But sitting down and being still in this context, it was hard for me to focus. I tried several times, but I failed to meditate on the imagery in the deep, dark valley of the shadow of death. The fear of darkness made it so difficult to meditate. I sensed an evil spirit or darkness engulfing my life. I could not feel a sense of peace and I was in deep fear. I felt goose-bumps, and it was very difficult for me to meditate on this verse. As soon as I pictured myself in the darkness, my mind seemed to drift into a state of deep fear.

I had some challenges learning to meditate on the first three verses of Psalm 23, but they were not as hard as this stage. I noticed that when I could not feel a sense of peace and tranquility while meditating on this verse, my heart was also pounding faster. The concept of a deep, dark valley affected my psychological being so profoundly. A sense of fear crept into my heart. I could not meditate. I was terrorized by the inside fears and terror of darkness. I also realized that it was not only the fear of the deep, dark valley that crippled me; the fear of meeting Comrades Hong and Hak also haunted my thinking, and disrupted my meditation. The images of these two evil men were stuck in my mind for many years after those incidents. As long as the pictures of these two men popped up in my mind, I felt psychologically crippled, and I could not explain the reason. I could never know how to explain why the images of these two evil men were so powerful in my life.

Once, in 1994, I wrote in my diary, "Why is it so hard for me to meditate on the deep, dark valley with the Shepherd of my soul? Why does my mind seem to be disturbed by the image of darkness and fear? Why does the fear of these two men haunt me like a ghost in my life? Why is it that I do not have a sense of peace and serenity when I meditate on verse four of Psalm 23?" As I closed my eyes to meditate on the concept of a sheep walking through the deep, dark valley of the shadow of death, it was not easy for me to meditate. I realized that the impact of psychological trauma had been affecting my life for many years. I kept reciting my prayer again and again:

Even though I walk in the valley of the shadow of death
I will fear no evil. The Shepherd of my soul is with me.
He will protect me. He is my Protector.

It was not difficult to keep repeating my prayer, but to envision myself as a sheep in the darkness, with the Shepherd of my soul, was very challenging. The fears inside me terrorized me and interrupted my meditation. My meditation was not at peace. I failed to remain still and know that my Shepherd was with me.

When fears inside attacked me, I could not meditate at all. I became unsettled. I could hardly bring myself closer to the Shepherd of my soul. After several months of meditation, I came to realize that it was not only psychological battles I was struggling with. It was also a spiritual battle. I had decided to focus on my meditation by taking more time to read the Bible. I prayed to my Shepherd to cast the fear out of me. I came to realize that my Shepherd was nearer to me than I thought: "for you are with me; your rod and your staff, they comfort me" (Psalm 23:4).

The Lord is my light and my salvation—
whom shall I fear?

The Lord is the stronghold of my life—
of whom shall I be afraid?
When the wicked advance against me to devour me,
it is my enemies and my foes who will stumble and fall.
Though an army besiege me, my heart will not fear;
though war break out against me,
even then I will be confident

(Psalm 27:1-3).

When I am afraid, I put my trust in you.
In God, whose word I praise—
in God I trust and am not afraid.
What can mere mortals do to me?

(Psalm 56:3-4)

Turn to me and be gracious to me,
for I am lonely and afflicted.
Relieve the troubles of my heart
and free me from my anguish.
Look on my affliction and my distress
and take away all my sins.
See how numerous are my enemies
and how fiercely they hate me!
Guard my life and rescue me;
do not let me be put to shame,
for I take refuge in you.

(Psalm 25:16-20)

PRAYER:

Lord, Shepherd of my soul, You are worthy of praise, and You are my Protector. I need to come closer to You. I realize that my mind is disturbed by the fears inside me. These fears have been controlling my life for many years. They have consumed my life. I was lost in my fear. As soon as I imagine myself sitting in the deep, dark valley, the fears start to creep into my heart. My Shepherd, You are my Fortress, and my Defender. I trust in You. I cannot function in my meditation. Please help me, Shepherd of my soul, to come to Your refuge. Help me to overcome my fears. Help me to feel a sense of peace and serenity as I learn to walk courageously with You, the Shepherd of my soul. Help me to cast out my fears or to dismiss the fears inside me. Help me to examine these fears and replace them with courage. I pray in the name of Jesus Christ, the Shepherd of my soul. Amen.

I think that verse 4 of Psalm 23 was the most challenging part of my journey in learning to meditate. The deep root of fear inside me crippled my life for many years, ever since my family was killed. I was not aware that being psychologically crippled later affected my ability to fight the spiritual battle. It took me about five years to learn how to overcome the fears inside me. I sat down and imagined myself sitting in the deep, dark valley, reciting, "Shepherd of my soul, I trust You, trust that You are with me. I know that Your rod and staff protect me. I shall fear no evil." I recited this sentence again and again. I admit that it is not easy to learn to overcome the fears. It will never come naturally, but I must learn to rely on the Shepherd of my soul, day by day.

I would like to end this part of the meditation with Psalm 91:1-16.

Whoever dwells in the shelter of the Most High
will rest in the shadow of the Almighty.
I will say of the LORD, "He is my refuge and my fortress,
my God, in whom I trust."
Surely, he will save you from the fowler's snare
and from the deadly pestilence.
He will cover you with his feathers,
and under his wings you will find refuge;
his faithfulness will be your shield and rampart.
You will not fear the terror of night,
nor the arrow that flies by day,
nor the pestilence that stalks in the darkness,
nor the plague that destroys at midday.
A thousand may fall at your side,
ten thousand at your right hand,
but it will not come near you.
You will only observe with your eyes
and see the punishment of the wicked.
If you say, "The LORD is my refuge,"
and you make the Most High your dwelling,
no harm will overtake you,
no disaster will come near your tent.
For he will command his angels concerning you
to guard you in all your ways;
they will lift you up in their hands,
so that you will not strike your foot against a stone.
You will tread on the lion and the cobra;
you will trample the great lion
and the serpent. "Because he loves me," says the Lord,

"I will rescue him; I will protect him,
for he acknowledges my name.
He will call on me, and I will answer him;
I will be with him in trouble,
I will deliver him and honor him.
With long life I will satisfy him
and show him my salvation."

Psalm 91 has become my personal Psalm of prayer when my family travels anywhere. Before we travel, we read this Psalm together and pray before we leave home. It reminds us that, though our trip may be unpredictable, we are travelling a life of communion with the Shepherd of our souls as a family. We are constantly safe under His protection, and may therefore be at peace, serene and secure. We are dwelling in the secret place of the protection of this Good Shepherd, and we shall abide under the shadow of the Almighty. We know that life is unpredictable, but by faith we look to the Shepherd to protect us. We choose this Shepherd to be our Refuge, Protector, and Defender. After we read this Psalm and pray for our trip, we feel safe and at peace when we travel.

It took me a long time to pray to cast out the spirit of darkness from me. I also got some friends to pray for me. It was not only psychological disturbance that made my meditation become difficult, it was also spiritual darkness I was wrestling with for many years. After I overcame my spiritual darkness, I could feel a sense of stillness and I knew that my Shepherd was with me. He guided me and protected me in my darkness. His rod and staff were with me.

MY PERSONAL REFLECTION

Life in the deep, dark valley is not the end,
but it is the beginning of the transformation

As I reflected on Psalm 23:4, I understood the deep, dark valley is the most fearful place to be in. No one wants to stay there. When I think about the deep, dark valley of my life, I will never forget the three nights in the deep, dark jungle after my family was killed. I stayed in the jungle near the graves of my family because I did not know what else to do. I was just a young boy; I did not fully understand what was going on. I was left alone without protection. Being alone in the jungle was terrifying for me.

The first night after my family was killed, I needed to climb up a tree and stay in it for the whole night. It was so dark. I could not see anything. I could hear the sounds of wild animals walking on the ground. I was terrified of the darkness. My hands were so shaky, I could hardly cling on to the tree. Many years later, I learned how deeply the psychological impact of the terror of being alone penetrated my life. Whenever I was alone in the jungle, I could feel the chill of being fearful again. My terror of being alone in the jungle haunted my mind and sent a terrible fear into my spine.

I have learned many lessons about the deep, dark valley of my life. All of us have stories to tell about the deep, dark valleys of our lives. Some of us can handle it positively while others end up in tragedy. When our prayers were not answered, we felt hopeless. It seemed as though the sky was falling on the deep, dark valley of our lives. It is the place of failure, the place of hopelessness, the place of fears, the place we feel utterly crushed emotionally and psychologically, and the place of pain we do not want. As I look at the biblical stories, I note there are some important ones that help me to learn more about the deep, dark valley.

There is the story of Joseph in Genesis 40-50. He was a young, handsome teenager. His father, Jacob, loved him dearly. In the modern world, we would say that his father favoured him and spoiled him. Jacob made his love known by dressing Joseph more finely than the rest of his children. It created a lot of jealousy among Joseph's older brothers. In fact, they hated him so deeply that they eventually plotted to kill him. They dropped him into a pit to let him die, but one of them decided that was not right and convinced the others to sell him to be a slave in Egypt instead.

What was it like for Joseph to be betrayed by his own brothers? Joseph was suddenly in the deep, dark valley of his life. He was afraid and hurt. He was sold by his brothers. He was taken out of his culture. He became a slave in a different culture. He could not speak their language. He knew nothing of the new customs. He was lonely in a strange culture. If you were in Joseph's shoes, how would you feel? He was in deep darkness. His trouble did not end there. Joseph was well-built and very handsome. His master's wife fell in love with him and wanted him to sleep with her. He refused again and again. He held onto his God-given moral standards by not betraying his master. In the end, he was falsely accused of sexual misconduct and was put in prison. His life was getting worse. In prison, his fellow inmate (the chief cupbearer to the king) made promises to him to get him out of prison should he himself be released. But when he got out, he forgot about Joseph. He was left behind in the prison. I believe that Joseph became desperate in his life. But he had learned earlier in his life to remain faithful to the Lord. He learned to discern God's presence and resist all temptations. He did not allow his life to be buried in the deep, dark valley of his life. In fact, his life was transformed in deep, dark valleys.

Later he became the second-highest man after Pharaoh. This is what he said to his brothers,

> *"You intended to harm me, but God intended it for good to accomplish what is now being done, the saving of many lives"* (Genesis 50:20).

It is hard to put ourselves in Joseph's shoes. We do not want to be transformed in the deep, dark valley of our lives. We sit and lament that our journey is not smooth and easy. We do not want to be disrupted by pain. We do not sign up for trials. We just want a simple, smooth journey. We want success. We do not want to talk about suffering. After many years of living in darkness, I learned to contemplate this verse from Paul:

> *And we know that in all things God works for the good of those who love him, who have been called according to **his** purpose* (Romans 8:28).

I think that this verse is one of the most popular quotations in the Bible, regarding how we handle our trials. A lot of people would think this verse is helpful in learning how to handle trials that inevitably hit us. People would use it to comfort themselves. They would say, "Don't worry, be happy; your loss isn't really so bad. Good things will come soon." Or, "One door is closed and another door will be opened for you." Many people would try their best to create a positive attitude while facing tribulation in life. I was not so sure what they would think if their situation got worse and worse. Would they remain faithful? Would they keep their positive attitude?

In my own journey, I learned more about my life in the deep, dark valley than I learned on a smooth road—an easy life. In my trials I learned more about the Shepherd of my soul. I learned to surrender to my Shepherd and to depend on His sufficient grace. I came across this verse so many times. Many years later, I realized that it was not the question "What happened in my life?" but it was "Where do I stand at the end?" I kept asking myself when I came through, out of my darkness, "Do I remain faithful to my Shepherd?"

The story of Daniel in Chapter 6:

It pleased Darius to appoint 120 satraps to rule throughout the kingdom, with three administrators over them, one of whom was Daniel. The satraps were made accountable to them so that the king might not suffer loss. Now Daniel so distinguished himself among the administrators and the satraps by his exceptional qualities that the king planned to set him over the whole kingdom. At this, the administrators and the satraps tried to find grounds for charges against Daniel in his conduct of government affairs, but they were unable to do so. They could find no corruption in him, because he was trustworthy and neither corrupt nor negligent. Finally, these men said, "We will never find any basis

175

for charges against this man Daniel unless it has something to do with the law of his God."

So, these administrators and satraps went as a group to the king and said: "May King Darius live forever! The royal administrators, prefects, satraps, advisers and governors have all agreed that the king should issue an edict and enforce the decree that anyone who prays to any god or human being during the next thirty days, except to you, Your Majesty, shall be thrown into the lions' den. Now, Your Majesty, issue the decree and put it in writing so that it cannot be altered—in accordance with the law of the Medes and Persians, which cannot be repealed." So, King Darius put the decree in writing.

Now when Daniel learned that the decree had been published, he went home to his upstairs room where the windows opened toward Jerusalem. Three times a day he got down on his knees and prayed, giving thanks to his God, just as he had done before. Then these men went as a group and found Daniel praying and asking God for help. So, they went to the king and spoke to him about his royal decree: "Did you not publish a decree that during the next thirty days anyone who prays to any god or human being except to you, Your Majesty, would be thrown into the lions' den?"

The king answered, "The decree stands—in accordance with the law of the Medes and Persians, which cannot be repealed."

Then they said to the king, "Daniel, who is one of the exiles from Judah, pays no attention to you, Your

Majesty, or to the decree you put in writing. He still prays three times a day." When the king heard this, he was greatly distressed; he was determined to rescue Daniel and made every effort until sundown to save him.

Then the men went as a group to King Darius and said to him, "Remember, Your Majesty, that according to the law of the Medes and Persians no decree or edict that the king issues can be changed."

So, the king gave the order, and they brought Daniel and threw him into the lions' den. The king said to Daniel, "May your God, whom you serve continually, rescue you!"

A stone was brought and placed over the mouth of the den, and the king sealed it with his own signet ring and with the rings of his nobles, so that Daniel's situation might not be changed. Then the king returned to his palace and spent the night without eating and without any entertainment being brought to him. And he could not sleep.

At the first light of dawn, the king got up and hurried to the lions' den. When he came near the den, he called to Daniel in an anguished voice, "Daniel, servant of the living God, has your God, whom you serve continually, been able to rescue you from the lions?"

Daniel answered, "May the king live forever! My God sent his angel, and he shut the mouths of the lions. They have not hurt me, because I was found innocent in his sight. Nor have I ever done any wrong before you, Your Majesty."

The king was overjoyed and gave orders to lift Daniel out of the den. And when Daniel was lifted from the den, no wound was found on him, because he had trusted in his God.

At the king's command, the men who had falsely accused Daniel were brought in and thrown into the lions' den, along with their wives and children. And before they reached the floor of the den, the lions overpowered them and crushed all their bones.

Then King Darius wrote to all the nations and peoples of every language in all the earth: "May you prosper greatly! I issue a decree that in every part of my kingdom people must fear and reverence the God of Daniel. For he is the living God and he endures forever; his kingdom will not be destroyed, his dominion will never end. He rescues and he saves; he performs signs and wonders in the heavens and on the earth. He has rescued Daniel from the power of the lions."

So, Daniel prospered during the reign of Darius and the reign of Cyrus the Persian.

Daniel was known to be a man faithful in prayer. Every day, he prayed three times. His enemies set spies upon him, to observe him in the management of his work; they sought to find something to hold against him, any mistakes on which to ground an accusation concerning the kingdom, some instance of neglect or partiality. But they could not find any misconduct against him. In the end, his enemies set up a dirty trap against him by introducing a decree against him. Daniel knew that his enemies tried to find a trap to accuse him, but he still got down on his knees and prayed three times a day, giving thanks to his God, just as he had done before.

Finally, his enemies succeeded by putting Daniel in the lion's den for a special treat for the starved lions. The biblical account does not give a detailed account of what Daniel did immediately after he was put in the lion's den, but I believe he probably felt fear and despair. He was in a deep, dark den. I think that he spent the whole night praying to the Lord. The Lord heard Daniel's prayer and sent the angel to shut the lions' mouths.

There are more stories like this in the Bible. For example, Jonah was in the fish's belly for three nights. Jonah was a prophet commanded by God to bring a message to Nineveh. Instead of obeying God's call to go there, Jonah ran away from the Lord and headed for Tarshish, which is in the exact opposite direction. The story gets really interesting. He ended up in a fish's belly. I like to eat fish, but I cannot stand the smell of fish. I can't really imagine what it is like to be in a fish's belly for three days. Jonah hit the bottom of his life—the deepest, darkest place in his life. But in the deepest, darkest place he cried out to God for help:

> From inside the fish Jonah prayed to the LORD his God. He said: "In my distress I called to the Lord, and he answered me. From deep in the realm of the dead I called for help, and you listened to my cry. You hurled me into the depths, into the very heart of the seas, and the currents swirled about me; all your waves and breakers swept over me. I said, 'I have been banished from your sight; yet I will look again toward your holy temple.' The engulfing waters threatened me, the deep surrounded

*me; seaweed was wrapped around my head. To the roots
of the mountains I sank down; the earth beneath barred
me in forever. But you, LORD my God, brought my life
up from the pit."*

(Jonah 2:1-6)

God caused the fish to literally vomit Jonah onto the
dry land. Jonah was transformed by the whole experience.

Peter rejected Christ three times. During Jesus' last
supper with His disciples, He predicted that Peter would
deny knowing Him three times, and after the third denial
Peter heard the rooster crow and recalled the prediction as
Jesus turned to look at him. Peter then began to cry bitterly. Here is the story of Peter's rejection of Jesus:

*Then Jesus told them, "This very night you will all fall
away on account of me, for it is written: 'I will strike the
shepherd, and the sheep of the flock will be scattered.'
But after I have risen, I will go ahead of you into
Galilee."*

*Peter replied, "Even if all fall away on account of you, I
never will."*

*"Truly I tell you," Jesus answered, "this very night,
before the rooster crows, you will disown me three times."*

*But Peter declared, "Even if I have to die with you, I will
never disown you."*

*And all the other disciples said the same. Then Jesus
went with his disciples to a place called Gethsemane,
and he said to them, "Sit here while I go over there and
pray."*

He took Peter and the two sons of Zebedee along with him, and he began to be sorrowful and troubled. Then he said to them, "My soul is overwhelmed with sorrow to the point of death. Stay here and keep watch with me." Going a little farther, he fell with his face to the ground and prayed, "My Father, if it is possible, may this cup be taken from me. Yet not as I will, but as you will." Then he returned to his disciples and found them sleeping. "Couldn't you men keep watch with me for one hour?" he asked Peter. "Watch and pray so that you will not fall into temptation. The spirit is willing, but the flesh is weak."

He went away a second time and prayed, "My Father, if it is not possible for this cup to be taken away unless I drink it, may your will be done." When he came back, he again found them sleeping, because their eyes were heavy. So he left them and went away once more and prayed the third time, saying the same thing. Then he returned to the disciples and said to them, "Are you still sleeping and resting? Look, the hour has come, and the Son of Man is delivered into the hands of sinners. Rise! Let us go! Here comes my betrayer!"

While he was still speaking, Judas, one of the Twelve, arrived. With him was a large crowd armed with swords and clubs, sent from the chief priests and the elders of the people. Now the betrayer had arranged a signal with them: "The one I kiss is the man; arrest him." Going at once to Jesus, Judas said, "Greetings, Rabbi!" and kissed him.

Jesus replied, "Do what you came for, friend." Then the men stepped forward, seized Jesus and arrested him. With that, one of Jesus' companions reached for his sword, drew it out and struck the servant of the high priest, cutting off his ear.

"Put your sword back in its place," Jesus said to him, "for all who draw the sword will die by the sword. Do you think I cannot call on my Father, and he will at once put at my disposal more than twelve legions of angels? But how then would the Scriptures be fulfilled that say it must happen in this way?"

In that hour Jesus said to the crowd, "Am I leading a rebellion, that you have come out with swords and clubs to capture me? Every day I sat in the temple courts teaching, and you did not arrest me. But this has all taken place that the writings of the prophets might be fulfilled." Then all the disciples deserted him and fled.

Those who had arrested Jesus took him to Caiaphas the high priest, where the teachers of the law and the elders had assembled. But Peter followed him at a distance, right up to the courtyard of the high priest. He entered and sat down with the guards to see the outcome.

The chief priests and the whole Sanhedrin were looking for false evidence against Jesus so that they could put him to death. But they did not find any, though many false witnesses came forward.

Finally, two came forward and declared, "This fellow said, 'I am able to destroy the temple of God and rebuild it in three days.'"

Then the high priest stood up and said to Jesus, "Are you not going to answer? What is this testimony that these men are bringing against you?"

But Jesus remained silent.

The high priest said to him, "I charge you under oath by the living God: Tell us if you are the Messiah, the Son of God."

"You have said so," Jesus replied. "But I say to all of you: From now on you will see the Son of Man sitting at the right hand of the Mighty One and coming on the clouds of heaven."

Then the high priest tore his clothes and said, "He has spoken blasphemy! Why do we need any more witnesses? Look, now you have heard the blasphemy. What do you think?"

"He is worthy of death," they answered.

Then they spit in his face and struck him with their fists. Others slapped him and said, "Prophesy to us, Messiah. Who hit you?"

Now Peter was sitting out in the courtyard, and a servant girl came to him. "You also were with Jesus of Galilee," she said.

But he denied it before them all. "I don't know what you're talking about," he said.

Then he went out to the gateway, where another servant girl saw him and said to the people there, "This fellow was with Jesus of Nazareth." He denied it again, with an oath: "I don't know the man!"

After a little while, those standing there went up to Peter and said, "Surely you are one of them; your accent gives you away." Then he began to call down curses, and he swore to them, "I don't know the man!"

Immediately a rooster crowed. Then Peter remembered the word Jesus had spoken: "Before the rooster crows, you will disown me three times." And he went outside and wept bitterly (Matthew 26:31-75).

What was it like for Peter to see his Master being falsely accused and beaten and insulted? What was going on in his heart? Peter was afraid Jesus would die, and he was fearful for his own life as well. The world hated Jesus, and Peter found that he was not prepared to face the ridicule and persecution that Jesus was suffering. Peter quickly found he wasn't nearly as bold and courageous as he had proclaimed. In fear, he denied knowing Jesus, who loved him.

Peter was in darkness, but he did not allow darkness to consume his life. He was later transformed to be the Rock. He became the pillar of the early Church in Jerusalem, exhorting and training others to follow the Lord Jesus. He wrote two epistles (1 and 2 Peter) to encourage others. Many preachers would like to conclude Peter's story like this, "God used Peter's many failures, including his three denials of Christ, to turn him from Simon, a common man with a common name, into Peter, the Rock.

The story of Paul's conversion is the most compelling story. He was known as the most fearful executioner in the early history of Christianity. He spent possibly half of his life persecuting Christians. Then, he obtained permission from the high priest to go to the synagogues in Damascus to persecute Christians. Here is the story of how he was blinded and so stricken that he could not eat for three days:

> Meanwhile, Saul was still breathing out murderous threats against the Lord's disciples. He went to the high priest and asked him for letters to the synagogues in Damascus, so that if he found any there who belonged to the Way, whether men or women, he might take them as prisoners to Jerusalem. As he neared Damascus on his journey, suddenly a light from heaven flashed around him. He fell to the ground and heard a voice say to him, "Saul, Saul, why do you persecute me?"
>
> "Who are you, Lord?" Saul asked.
>
> "I am Jesus, whom you are persecuting," he replied. "Now get up and go into the city, and you will be told what you must do." The men travelling with Saul stood there speechless; they heard the sound but did not see anyone. Saul got up from the ground, but when he opened his eyes he could see nothing. So they led him by the hand into Damascus. For three days he was blind, and did not eat or drink anything.
>
> In Damascus there was a disciple named Ananias. The Lord called to him in a vision, "Ananias!"
>
> "Yes, Lord," he answered.
>
> The Lord told him, "Go to the house of Judas on Straight Street and ask for a man from Tarsus named Saul, for he is praying. In a vision he has seen a man named Ananias come and place his hands on him to restore his sight."

"Lord," Ananias answered, "I have heard many reports about this man and all the harm he has done to your holy people in Jerusalem. And he has come here with authority from the chief priests to arrest all who call on your name."

But the Lord said to Ananias, "Go! This man is my chosen instrument to proclaim my name to the Gentiles and their kings and to the people of Israel. I will show him how much he must suffer for my name."

Then Ananias went to the house and entered it. Placing his hands on Saul, he said, "Brother Saul, the Lord—Jesus, who appeared to you on the road as you were coming here—has sent me so that you may see again and be filled with the Holy Spirit." Immediately, something like scales fell from Saul's eyes, and he could see again. He got up and was baptized, and after taking some food, he regained his strength (Acts 9:1-19).

As a general who was in charge of a group of soldiers, what was it like for Paul to become blind for three days? All his men deserted him. Was he afraid that his enemy would come to take his life? What could he do to prevent himself from being killed? None of his men stayed with him to protect him. He was in darkness. Later he was transformed. Even though he was locked in prison waiting for a fair trial, he managed to write letters to encourage other believers.

Life in a deep, dark valley is the most fearful place for all of us. No one wants to go there, and no one wants to suffer. No one wants to go through the deep, dark valley. No one wants a hard life. No one wants to be pruned. I never wanted to stay in the deep, dark valley, but it is where I needed the Shepherd the most and it was where the transformation of my life began. Life in darkness is not the end, but it is where the transformation begins. The resurrection of my Good Shepherd began in the dark tomb.

I realize now that the moment I hit the bottom of the deep, dark valley, I began to build the foundation of my Christian faith. At the bottom I learned to build up my trust in my Shepherd. I know that my Shepherd promised His children that He would never leave them or forsake them (Joshua 1:5). This is the promise from the Shepherd in times of difficult circumstances. In my trial the promise that my Shepherd would never forsake me was a huge comfort, but this comfort would never come easily or naturally. Many times I questioned in my heart where my Shepherd was when I needed Him most. I wrestled in my heart about His silence. He did not answer my prayer as quickly as I had hoped. He did not always reveal Himself to me as dramatically as I would've liked Him to. Nor did He always answer my prayer immediately.

Sometimes I did not want to read His Word anymore. At some points I wanted to avoid fellowship with others. I simply wanted to be alone. I just wanted to be by myself and I did not want to be disturbed by anyone. It took me time to come to realize that my Shepherd is always with me. He wants me to stay connected with Him. He wants me to talk to Him more and more. He is here with me, but He is silent. He waits to hear from me. His promise is a huge comfort in my heart. I may not see Him. I may not feel His presence, but one thing I keep in my heart: my Shepherd never forsakes me. He is there for me and He never leaves me. I need to recognize that His grace is sufficient for me.

No matter what happens to me, I try my best to keep my focus on the Shepherd of my soul by not derailing from Him.

I am writing this part during the COVID-19 pandemic (March 2020). People around the world are paralyzed by fear of this virus. COVID-19 shocks and shakes the world. When COVID-19 first happened in China, not many world leaders could have imagined that the virus would eventually spread throughout the world. I was in Cambodia, planning a trip for speaking engagements in New Zealand. My friend Pastor Henry Wong had arranged for me to speak there. I booked my two-way tickets from Phnom Penh to Auckland through Malaysian Airlines.

About twenty-seven days before my departure, the airline wrote to me saying that they had to cancel my return ticket from Auckland to Phnom Penh. Besides the tickets being cancelled, I also had trouble with a gallstone. The pain hit me during the night. It was very painful. I went to see two specialists in Siem Reap's private clinic and Surin hospital in Thailand. The gallstone was very small, only 0.3 cm. They decided not to do surgery at this stage. Eventually I decided to change my ticket to return to Toronto instead, to be with my family in the time of fear of COVID-19.

When I arrived in Toronto, only thirty-seven people were infected by this virus in Canada, but six months after that, the infection total rose to more than two hundred thousand people, with more than ten thousand dead. The whole country became paralyzed by the fear of this virus. Many people in Canada and around the world flooded to the malls to buy food supplies and toilet paper. People constantly focused on the news on TV or Facebook and newspapers. I read so much news on social media. I concluded that it was the world's worst physical and psychological threat of the twenty-first century. The fear of COVID-19 is real. It sent shockwaves around the world. Schools, sports clubs, churches, restaurants, factories, and public gatherings were all shut down by the individual governments around the world. My friend Pastor James Lee sent me a message that described the shockwave of the world's fear:

"I don't know who wrote this, but it's beautiful.

'We fell asleep in one world and woke up in another.
Suddenly Disney is out of magic.
Paris is no longer romantic.
New York doesn't stand up anymore,
the Chinese wall is no longer a fortress, and Mecca is empty.
Hugs and kisses suddenly become weapons,
and not visiting parents and friends becomes an act of love.
Suddenly you realize that power, beauty and money
are worthless,
and can't get you the oxygen you're fighting for.
The world continues its life and it is beautiful.
It only puts humans in cages.
I think it's sending us a message."

People are constantly fearful of the unseen enemy we call COVID-19. This fear cripples not only psychologically, but also economically around the world too. The Canadian government declared a state of emergency. They decided to inject more than three hundred billion dollars into the state of emergency funds to maintain the economy and fight against the COVID-19 pandemic. They eventually decided to close the borders to prevent travellers infected with the virus from entering Canada. It is hard to fight an unseen enemy. We do not know when and where they will attack us. It has been the terrible fear of the century. When we are called to confront a visible enemy, we can stand in unity to fight against them. Now, fighting against an invisible enemy, we are not called to stand in unity, but to stay apart. It is our best strategy to stop the spread of infection. Our Canadian Prime Minister, Justin Trudeau, urged, "Let's save lives together by staying apart."

Our government indicated that Canadians had contracted the disease while travelling in other countries all over the world. Certain cases in Canada, which were linked to travel, had led to human-to-human transmission between close contacts. The Canadian government encouraged all Canadians to practice social distancing—keeping space between yourself and other people outside of your home. Social distancing has proven to be one of the most effective ways to reduce the spread of illness during the COVID-19 pandemic. It is the only strategy to stop the spread of the virus from human-to-human transmission at this point in time. The biggest fear is that we do not know when the whole world could defeat this deadly invisible enemy. It creates only high anxiety, fear, worry, and depression. The worst thing about this virus attack is that we cannot be with our loved ones while they are dying or have a normal funeral for them. We cannot spend their last moments saying a proper farewell. We feel very sad for the victims of COVID-19.

My wife and I went for a walk in a public park for at least five kilometres a day, just to get out of the house for fresh air. Our government allowed us to walk outside, but we had to stay at least two metres apart for social distancing. I could see that more cars were parked in front of the houses and along the roads than there used to be. People were asked to stay inside their homes. The psychological fear was intensified across the whole country for months. Many people became depressed by the fear of this virus. Now as I write this at the end of 2020, we are more than nine months into the pandemic. The virus has infected almost one hundred million people worldwide, killing almost two million people. It has been a big shock to the whole world, and the worst thing is that scientists and medical doctors still do not have an effective vaccine to fight against this virus. We do not know when we can defeat the virus COVID-19.

There were so many theories (some of them myths) on how to prevent infection from COVID-19. The theories and myths spread around the world faster than the virus itself. The fear of COVID-19 has crept into the world and it has paralyzed the economy worldwide.

I spoke to several close friends who are Christians, living in a few different countries; they told me that they were terrified by COVID-19. They could not go to church and they could not resume a normal life. I encouraged them that it was now they needed the Lord the most; they needed to kneel down to pray to the Lord. It was not the end yet, but it was at this time they needed to learn to surrender to the Lord. It was time to begin to learn to be transformed from their deep, dark valley of life. I also received encouragement from my friend Pastor James Lee in this time of fear of the COVID-19 pandemic. He sent me this text:

"At this time of lockdown and shut down, we all need to search our hearts, humble ourselves, turn from our wicked ways and seek His face unceasingly. Let us only look to God for refuge and comfort. It's time for corrections for all people of the world. We have been too busy running events but not searching our hearts deep enough to repent and realign ourselves. We have sidelined God far too long, our being and souls need to pause to reflect and to realign. Our energy for loving God and people has been marginalized, causing humankind to be more self-centred and self-righteous; we worship power, lust, and wealth more than God. So, it's a wake-up call for myself and many other church leaders. We tend to be more institution-based than people-oriented. Most of us have lost the very purpose God intended for us. God has mercy on me and those who are in the front lines for God. My prayer is for all of us who are called to be children of God. Let us continue to be the Salt and Light of our community."

It is true that we need to turn our heart to the Shepherd for help. No matter what we have been going through, we need to keep in mind that our Shepherd is with us.

"When you pass through the waters, I will be with you; and when you pass through the rivers, they will not sweep over you. When you walk through the fire, you will not be burned; the flames will not set you ablaze" (Isaiah 43:2).

All we need to do is replace our fears with more prayers. We should focus less on what social media is saying, but pay more attention to reading the Bible and worshipping. In this stressful time, the more we spend time on social media, the more we will likely become depressed by the fear of invisible enemies.

For all of us in our own journey, there is a deep, dark valley of life. It comes to us unexpectedly and inevitably.

For me, I know what it meant to be in the deep, dark valley of my life. I had a secret fear that I would end up in a mental institute. The symptoms of PTSD, especially fear, depression, nightmares, and insomnia took control of my life for more than fifteen years. It made me so miserable.

Sometimes when I was in deep depression, I just wanted to have one good night's sleep, but it was beyond my reach. It was not just one day or one week that I could not sleep, but it had been too many long years. Mentally, I was about to collapse. There was a deep fear inside my heart. It was not only insomnia and nightmares that caused my concern. There were many more psychological symptoms such as depression, anxiety attacks, constant worries, headaches, hopelessness, feeling guilty, restlessness, anxiety, and difficulty concentrating too. It was extremely difficult for me to handle these psychological symptoms. I reached the point of breaking down. I thought that I would never be normal again. I was so worried that I would end up in a psychiatric institution. It was the worst secret fear that crept into my heart for many years. I could never tell anyone of my worst secret fear in my heart. This fear turned my normal life upside down.

Many years later, I realized that what I feared the most began to influence my heart—my heart was absolutely controlled by the fear. Whatever I did in my life, this fear influenced my heart. *"Above all else, guard your heart, for everything you do flows from it"* (Proverbs 4:23). It was true that the fear inside me flowed from my heart. I failed to guard my heart. I unconsciously allowed my heart to be controlled by the fear that I would end up in a psychiatric institution.

Then, this fear became my spiritual warfare. It was my spiritual battle between fear and faith. I must honestly admit that my faith was not strong enough to conquer the fear inside my heart. When the symptoms of PTSD choked my life, I asked where the Shepherd of my soul was when I was so desperately in need of help. During my struggle as a Christian, I learned that my heart was a battleground between fear and faith. When my faith was weak, I yelled to my Shepherd, "Where were You when I needed You the most?" He was far from my reach. He did not listen to my cry for help. He was not caring for me. When I was at the peak of fear, I became confused.

However, this fear motivated me to study counselling and psychology. My main purpose in studying this was to educate myself about the impact of PTSD and how it affected my thinking and behaviour. I spent a lot of time doing my own research on PTSD. The more I learned about it, the more I became worried that I might end up in a psychiatric institution. There was no magical solution for PTSD. There were many theories and suggestions on how to cope with it. My own knowledge helped me to learn to cope with my symptoms. It also helped me to be aware of my behaviour.

My personal research helped me to understand myself, but the healing grace came from the Shepherd of my soul. I learned a lot about the meaning of life in the times of my troubles. I have learned that the deep, dark valley of my life was the place I needed to learn to depend on the Shepherd of my soul the most. It was the place where I needed to learn to be transformed from the dark- ness of my life to the light of life my Shepherd intended for me. It was in that place I realized that I desperately needed healing grace from my Shepherd to heal my psychological wounds and my broken spirit.

It was not easy for me to learn, because transformation began with pain and suffering. A smooth ride would never help my life grow in my faith. Without acknowledging the pain, I would never clearly understand the abundance of life the Shepherd of my soul provided when He came to die for my sin on the Cross.

Every time I conducted a Communion service at church, I could not hold back my tears as I reflected on the moment the Shepherd of my soul bore my sin on the Cross. He gave His life for me on the Cross. He took the condemnation I deserved and offered me forgiveness. I never deserved to be set free, but He did set me free indeed. The pain my Shepherd bore for me was so tremendous that I could never pay back what he did for me there. I can only respond with my utmost gratitude and thanksgiving to this great Shepherd. My suffering in life is so insignificant when compared to the suffering of the Shepherd of my soul, who died on the Cross to pay for my sin. I am so grateful for what He has done for me!

Sometimes, I sensed that the Shepherd of my soul was far from me, that He did not hear my prayers. I thought that He was not interested in listening to my pain and that he had left me in the deep, dark valley of life by myself. I became desperate in my deep depression. This spiritual battle of fear and faith in my life kept pushing and pulling me like a tug of war. For years my life was defined by deep fear. It was the result of weak faith. This weak faith produced doubt in my mind. I was a young Christian just converted from Buddhism.

I realized that no one begins as a mature Christian. I had a lot to learn to absorb more Christian principles and knowledge and grow in faith. I spent six years at Christian schools, learning about my faith. Even graduating from Christian schools did not mean I automatically became more mature in my Christian faith. What I learned at these schools was just head knowledge, not the heart of the Christian faith.

Like so many Christians, when doubt crept into my life, I began to question or wonder where my Shepherd was in the time of my darkness. Was my Shepherd with me in the time of my need? Were His rod and staff really protecting me? Sometimes I got up in the middle of the night, and I would think that this Shepherd did not make sense to me. I pondered whether I should bring my doubt to Him. I had spent time reading the Book of Psalms. I could see David had gone through a lot of doubts about God. He wrote many Psalms when he had his doubts in God:

Answer me when I call to you, my righteous God. Give me relief from my distress; have mercy on me and hear my prayer.

(Psalm 4:1)

Lord, do not rebuke me in your anger or discipline me in your wrath. Have mercy on me, Lord, for I am faint; heal me, Lord, for my bones are in agony. My soul is in deep anguish. How long, Lord, how long?

Turn, Lord, and deliver me; save me because of your unfailing love. Among the dead, no one proclaims your name. Who praises you from the grave? I am worn out from my groaning. All night long I flood my bed with weeping and drench my couch with tears. My eyes grow weak with sorrow; they fail because of all my foes.

Away from me, all you who do evil, for the Lord has heard my weeping. The Lord has heard my cry for mercy; the Lord accepts my prayer. All my enemies will be overwhelmed with shame and anguish; they will turn back and suddenly be put to shame.

(Psalm 6:1-10)

Lord my God, I take refuge in you; save and deliver me from all who pursue me, or they will tear me apart like a lion and rip me to pieces with no one to rescue me.

(Psalm 7:1-2)

My God, my God, why have you forsaken me? Why are you so far from saving me, so far from my cries of anguish? My God, I cry out by day, but you do not answer, by night, but I find no rest.

(Psalm 22:1-2)

Vindicate me, my God, and plead my cause against an unfaithful nation. Rescue me from those who are deceitful and wicked. You are God my stronghold. Why have you rejected me? Why must I go about mourning, oppressed by the enemy? Send me your light and your faithful care, let them lead me; let them bring me to your holy mountain, to the place where you dwell. Then I will go to the altar of God, to God, my joy and my delight. I will praise you with the lyre, O God, my God.

Why, my soul, are you downcast? Why so disturbed within me? Put your hope in God for I will yet praise him, my Savior, and my God.

(Psalm 43:1-5)

Hear my prayer, Lord; let my cry for help come to you.
Do not hide your face from me when I am in distress.
Turn your ear to me; when I call, answer me quickly.
For my days vanish like smoke;
my bones burn like glowing embers.
My heart is blighted and withered like grass;
I forget to eat my food. In my distress, I groan aloud
and am reduced to skin and bones.
I am like a desert owl, like an owl among the ruins.
I lie awake; I have become like a bird alone on a roof.
All-day long my enemies taunt me;
those who rail against me use my name as a curse.
For I eat ashes as my food and mingle my drink with tears
because of your great wrath,
for you have taken me up and thrown me aside.
My days are like the evening shadow;
I wither away like grass.

(Psalm 102:1-11)

These Psalms were written when David was doubting his God the way I did. Most Psalms are written in times of personal crisis of faith. Many trials in his life caused David to feel that his Shepherd was far from him and had abandoned him. He cried out for help, but the Shepherd did not answer his prayers. David never gave up seeking his Shepherd. His doubts drove him to seek Him wholeheartedly. He wanted to remain faithful to Him. He wanted to remain in the house of his Shepherd for the rest of his life. His doubt of his Shepherd was a simple sign of the struggle of faith in his life and yet he kept searching for Him. I personally think that it is a healthy sign to struggle with one's faith. I went through a lot of doubts in my life, but I never gave up searching for my Shepherd in my journey. I have remained faithful to Him even until now.

Some people, when they doubt God, drift away from Him. In my ministry in Cambodia, I baptized many people, but not all of them remained faithful to the Lord. Only thirty percent of them still remain worshipping the Lord. Seventy percent drifted away from Him. Those who left thought God was not worthy of their trust; they did not believe that they worshipped the living God, or they simply did not trust God anymore.

As a Christian, I learned that it was normal and healthy to doubt this Shepherd of my soul. It helped me to learn to seek Him more earnestly. I learned to build my faith in my Shepherd. It has taken me many years to learn to grow in my Christian faith, step by step. Spiritual warfare will never end, but I need to be ready to learn to rely on the Shepherd of my soul to walk with me through the deep, dark valleys of life. The only way I can learn to overcome my fear is to fear the Shepherd of my soul. *"Better a little with the fear of the Lord than great wealth with turmoil"* (Proverbs 15:16). I think that to fear the Shepherd of my soul would be a sure way to live to learn to overcome the worst secret fear. I need to try my best to move closer to my Shepherd and seek to build a good relationship with Him. My Shepherd will cast my fear away from me.

PRAYER:

Lord, Shepherd of my soul, You are my Defender, and my Fortress. I come to You in the midst of my fear. There are a lot of fears in my life. I fear my past trauma, nightmares, insomnia, and the secret fears of my life. In the midst of the deep, dark valley of life, I totally depend on You, the Shepherd of my soul. Only You can cast the fears from me.

I thank You that You have brought me through the deep, dark valley of life, and I have learned a great deal of lessons from the deep, dark valley of life. It was not the end of my journey, but it was my journey of learning to be transformed from darkness to light.

O Good Shepherd, You have restored my life. You have healed my brokenness. You have restored my health. You have given me peace.

"Peace I leave with you; my peace I give you. I do not give to you as the world gives. Do not let your hearts be troubled and do not be afraid" (John 14:27).

I personally thank You for the wonderful peace You have given me. No treasure is better than Your peace. Thank You for Your rod and staff that protect me in the deep, dark valley of my life. My beloved Shepherd, thank You for helping me to learn to depend on You when I was in doubt. Thank You for helping me to overcome my brokenness. You have restored my confidence. You have given me the wisdom to understand the impact of these traumas. You have led me to help others.

Shepherd of my soul, in the deep, dark valley of life, I absolutely depend on You. Shepherd of my soul, I thank

You that You are my Good Shepherd and You lay down Your life for me. I am forever grateful for what You have done for my life. Amen.

I would like to conclude with what Jesus said about Himself as the Shepherd who laid down His life for the sheep.

> "I am the good shepherd. The good shepherd lays down his life for the sheep. The hired hand is not the shepherd and does not own the sheep. So when he sees the wolf coming, he abandons the sheep and runs away. Then the wolf attacks the flock and scatters it. The man runs away because he is a hired hand and cares nothing for the sheep.

> "I am the good shepherd; I know my sheep and my sheep know me—just as the Father knows me and I know the Father—and I lay down my life for the sheep. I have other sheep that are not of this sheep pen. I must bring them also. They too will listen to my voice, and there shall be one flock and one shepherd. The reason my Father loves me is that I lay down my life—only to take it up again. No one takes it from me, but I lay it down of my own accord. I have authority to lay it down and authority to take it up again. This command I received from my Father."

> (John 10:11-18)

YOUR REVIEW & REFLECTION

1. In the deep, dark valley of your life, what do you see?

2. Who is your biggest enemy?

3. What do you want from your Shepherd?

4. Are you ever tempted to do things in your own way?

5. Have you ever doubted your Shepherd?

6. What has been the darkest time in your life?

7. What is your favourite way to avoid dealing with your dark valleys? Are you willing to give up that escape and trust God to walk with you through the valley?

8. Write down your prayers:

5

MY SHEPHERD PREPARES THE BANQUET TABLE

A call to face my enemies

N ow the journey shifts from the field of green pasture to the palace where David describes a banquet the Lord prepared for him in front of his enemies.

> *You prepare a table before me*
> *in the presence of my enemies.*
> *You anoint my head with oil; my cup overflows.*

(Psalm 23:5)

David might be sitting in the palace where the Lord provided him with a magnificent banquet, and he felt safe to sit down at the table with confidence, knowing that he was protected. He enjoyed his feast in perfect security without worrying. Perhaps many enemies surrounded him, but he was not concerned about them. His enemies could not touch him. David also knew the quality of food, which was abundant for him and perhaps his friends. The

Lord anointed him with oil. I like to think that "anoint my head with oil" might refer to anointing with joy, with the oil of joy that he writes about later.

You love righteousness and hate wickedness;
therefore God, your God,
has set you above your companions
by anointing you with the oil of joy.

(Psalm 45:7)

MY PERSONAL MEDITATION

My Shepherd prepares the feast
before my enemies

Before I started my meditation, I tried to relax. Relaxation is helpful for a meditation. Please refer to the previous chapter about the relaxation method. I would recite in my mind, "Shepherd of my soul, thank you for preparing the table before my enemies." Closing my eyes, reciting this phrase is not difficult for me—just to relax and spend about ten to fifteen minutes reciting this phrase, again and gain.

The focus of the meditation has now shifted from the green pastures to the palace. There are two pictures that I desire to paint in my mind. The first is a picture of myself at the table with my beloved Shepherd. I picture myself sitting at the table with abundant food on it. The host, who is my Shepherd, is sitting on one side waiting for me to come and sit with Him on the other side. It is an honour to come and join the feast with my Shepherd, but I feel unworthy as I examine myself. I know that I do not deserve such a feast of honour.

I have failed to earn the feast of honour because of my sin. I feel a sense of guilt and inability to stand before my Shepherd in His glorious holy presence. Paul indicated, *"For all have sinned and fall short of the glory of God"* (Romans 3:23). I feel that I do not deserve this feast of honour. Inside my heart, there is unresolved anger and bitterness. These negative emotions have stayed inside my heart for many years, boiling, ready to explode any time. I knew this anger was wrongly programmed in my mind since the day I saw my family killed. The impact of psychological trauma left me with a deep sense of anger inside me. This anger became a big ball of fire rolling inside my heart for years.

The pursuit of vengeance became the motive of my life. It had been crippling my life for years, and I kept living day by day, unwilling to deal with it. It was not healthy for me. Even though I had become a Christian, I did not know how to let it go. In fact, I did not have the courage to sit down with someone to tell him or her how deep the anger in my heart was. Indeed, I would feel ashamed to tell anyone about my anger. The best option for me seemed to be to keep it all bottled up tightly within my heart.

Paul said, *"In your anger do not sin: Do not let the sun go down while you are still angry"* (Ephesians 4:26).

What I have learned from this verse is that as a Christian, I may be angry. It is acceptable, but I should not allow the anger to govern my actions. I must not let the sun go down on my wrath. I heard a preacher say something like this, "If your anger implies resentment of an injury or ill-will and bitterness of spirit, you need to look to God for grace to enable you to be set free from this kind of anger. Do not carry your anger in your heart. It will eventually destroy you."

It was an important message that I heard from this preacher. From a psychological point of view, it is true that unresolved grief or anger can cause a lot more emotional and psychological damage and it would have eventually destroy my life. After doing some studies on the impact of PTSD, I was very much aware of my unresolved grief and anger. In fact, I was about to collapse.

I wish I could have let my anger go the day after my family was killed. But I could not let it go. I knew that the power of anger took control of my life, and created a lot of unresolved and unexpressed grief inside my heart. I could hardly go on living daily without being overwhelmed by my anger. To put it simply, I was a very angry man. Right after my family was killed, my anger stuck to my mind and soul like super glue. This anger influenced me with a desire of taking revenge for my family. At times, I was afraid that it would erupt like a volcano. Inside my heart, there was a giant ball of fire that I could not control. It could blow up any time.

Many years after my family was killed, I still embraced my bitterness. I was stuck in the darkness of sin. I failed to deal with my bitterness, and I allowed it to take control of my life.

"For I see that you are full of bitterness and captive to sin" (Acts 8:23).

The bitterness became cancer to my soul. When I allowed bitterness to fester in my life, I missed the healing grace of my Shepherd.

See to it that no one falls short of the grace of God and that no bitter root grows up to cause trouble and defile many (Hebrews 12:15).

Bitterness locked me into the dark side of life. It grew and bore the fruit of deep depression.

Seeing myself full of anger and bitterness, I felt unworthy to join my Shepherd at the table. My relationship with my Shepherd was not genuinely healthy. I was bruised by my broken spirit. My heart was full of sin. I did not deserve this feast of honour. My anger and bitterness were born out of the felt need of taking revenge for my family, to fulfill the pursuit of family honour. It robbed me of the joy of participating at the table with my Shepherd. It was blocking my relationship with Him.

"Each heart knows its own bitterness, and no one else can share its joy" (Proverbs 14:10). When I imagined sitting in front of my Shepherd I would feel guilty for allowing sin to infect my heart for so long. My anger and bitterness robbed me of the joy of having a good relationship with Him. I felt as though my spiritual growth was deeply hindered by my anger and bitterness. It was my broken spirit. It was the sin inside my heart. My spiritual health was hindered by my sin and bitterness.

David prayed,

Have mercy on me, O God, according to your unfailing love; according to your great compassion blot out my transgressions. Wash away all my iniquity and cleanse me from my sin. For I know my transgressions, and my sin is always before me.

(Psalm 51:1-3)

PRAYER:

Lord, Shepherd of my soul, You are my Rock, my Healer, and my Deliverer. I have tasted enough anger and bitterness in my life. I know that the root of anger and bitterness was born out of my unforgiving attitude toward my family's killers. It is very deep in my heart and soul, making it difficult to connect with You. I delayed putting my anger and bitterness out of my heart, and it has now taken a deep root inside my heart. I cannot pull it out of there. My anger has created a lot of heat inside my heart and the heat has burned me day after day. I have no peace inside my heart. My anger and bitterness bear only rotten fruit. It is not healthy for me. I cannot carry this rotten fruit in my body any longer. It blocks my personal relationship with You. I cannot come closer to You. I no longer want to keep the rotten fruit in my life.

Shepherd of my soul, I desperately need Your grace to get rid of the anger and bitterness from my heart. Enough is enough! Now I have finally made this decision to pull this rotten fruit out of my life. I need to replace it with healthy fruit. Help me to produce good fruit.

Shepherd of my soul, please grant me peace and cleanse my heart as we pull my anger out of my heart. I need to move on in newness of life. Shepherd of my soul, I call to You, my righteous One, please release me from my guilt and have mercy on me, and hear my prayer, as I have decided to uproot my anger and bitterness from my soul. Please help me to restore my relationship with You. Help me to come closer to You. Amen.

The second imagery I created in my mind was that I was sitting in front of my enemies. In my mind, I knew that I should not fear my enemies because I felt safe in front of my Shepherd. My enemies looked at me, but they could not destroy me because the Shepherd of my soul was protecting me. *"Truly my soul finds rest in God; my salvation comes from him. Truly he is my rock and my salvation; he is my fortress, I will never be shaken"* (Psalm 62:1-2). In the mighty hand of my Shepherd, I felt secure. My enemies could not come close to me. Learning to take refuge in the Shepherd of my soul was not difficult. I felt as though my soul was secure in the presence of my Shepherd. David wrote several Psalms when he felt secure in the Lord:

> *Keep me safe, my God, for in you I take refuge.*
> *I say to the LORD,*
> *"You are my LORD;*
> *apart from you I have no good thing."*
> *I say of the holy people who are in the land,*
> *"They are the noble ones in whom is all my delight."*
> *Those who run after other gods will suffer more and more.*
> *I will not pour out libations of blood*
> *to such gods or take up their names on my lips.*
> *Lord, you alone are my portion and my cup;*
> *you make my lot secure.*
>
> (Psalm 16:1-5)

> *I love you, LORD, my strength.*
> *The Lord is my rock, my fortress, and my deliverer;*
> *my God is my rock, in whom I take refuge, my shield,*
> *and the horn of my salvation, my stronghold.*
> *I called to the LORD, who is worthy of praise,*
> *and I have been saved from my enemies.*
>
> (Psalm 18:1-3)

211

Praise be to the LORD my Rock,
who trains my hands for war, my fingers for battle.
He is my loving God and my fortress,
my stronghold and my deliverer, my shield,
in whom I take refuge, who subdues peoples under me.

(Psalm 144:1-2)

But let all who take refuge in you be glad;
let them ever sing for joy.
Spread your protection over them, that those
who love your name may rejoice in you.
Surely, LORD, you bless the righteous;
you surround them with your favor as with a shield.

(Psalm 5:11-12)

MY PERSONAL REFLECTION

I cannot forget, but I have chosen
to forgive my enemies

As I contemplated the concept of participating in a feast of honour with the Shepherd of my soul, I realized that I was not worthy of joining Him as long as I still held onto my natural inclinations. It was not the way He intended me to live. I felt that my conscience was not correct as long as I still held onto my old self or my so-called personal instincts. This personal reflection on this part is a very serious personal self-examination. I must get rid of my anger and bitterness and learn to put on a new self, with which my Shepherd intends me to live.

As I looked back on the journey of my life from the grave to the present, I could see His amazing grace for my life. He had spared me from the Killing Fields. He had taken me on a long journey through the deep, dark valley of my life. He restored my health and gave me a new family of my own. He healed me from the symptoms of PTSD. He led me to meet many good people who helped me to grow in my journey. Now, my Shepherd has called me to meet my enemies and to forgive them. Could I do it? How could I handle my feelings?

To join the table with my Shepherd, I needed to behave the way my Shepherd wanted me to live, not the way I wanted to live. I was reminded that I was no longer the old me, but a new person in the Shepherd of my soul. I must live the way of the new life—not the way of the old self. Paul wrote to the Ephesians to encourage them to take away the worldly way of life and replace it with the new way of life from the teaching of Jesus:

> *When you heard about Christ and were taught in him in accordance with the truth that is in Jesus. You were taught, with regard to your former way of life, to put off your old self, which is being corrupted by its deceitful desires; to be made new in the attitude of your minds; and to put on the new self, created to be like God in true righteousness and holiness* (Ephesians 4:21-24).

My old life's goal was the pursuit of family honour—to take revenge for my family. The Cambodian culture of honour for the family deeply influenced my mental attitude. In fact, my mental attitude was corrupted by evil desire. The concept of the pursuit of my family honour kept boiling in my heart for years. I had to stop chasing my dream of taking revenge for my family. Most of all, I had to make a desperate attempt to change my old way of life. I had to learn to put on a new mental attitude—the mind of Christ in my life. It was a big challenge.

How could I forget those three days after my family was killed, when I knelt down in front of the graves and vowed to take revenge for them? Nothing else mattered to me except the longing to return to kill my enemies. How could I fail my family? How could I live with that disgrace? I was torn by two perspectives—my own human instincts and my new faith as a Christian. As I have examined my personal journey with the Shepherd of my soul, I have become aware that my personal growth was limited by the roots of my human instincts—the ways I wanted for my life. They were not the way that my Shepherd intended for me. I just wanted to do things according to my own instincts.

From the moment I walked out of the grave, I nurtured a desire to take revenge for my family. I got up early in the morning, and I nurtured in my heart that I would try my best to live so that I could return to fulfill my first promise. This mental attitude of taking revenge was deeply rooted in my heart for years. The concept of family honour had powerfully influenced my life. Failing to honour my family would bring disgrace. I could not accept the concept of losing face. Feeling guilty for failing to honour my family poked so deeply in my heart. I harboured anger and bitterness for years.

I did not know how to deal with my anger. I did not realize the extent of the anger and longing to take revenge had brought me—only anger, rage, bitterness, and no peace. The anger kept boiling in my heart, but I did not know how to tell anyone about it. From the outside, I looked so peaceful, but inside I was full of conflict, confusion, and insecurity. I unconsciously learned to embrace the anger and bitterness inside my heart and wouldn't let them go. In fact, I didn't know how. Emotionally, I was crippled. I tried to hide my feelings and control my anger, bitterness, and hurt. I suppressed all of these negative emotions to the point of numbness. It was hard to live with emotional numbness.

I learned that such emotional numbness affected every single part of my life. I lost the joy of life and was in a state of desperate despair. Any hope of moving forward was shrouded in darkness. Anger and bitterness ate my conscience alive. It was hard to live with such anger and bitterness. In order to handle it, I learned to suppress it, but in doing this over several years, I came to an impasse where I found I was emotionally numb. Living with this numbness necessitated pretending that nothing had happened to me, that I was not hurt badly.

I had lost my family and I felt as though my life was still overwhelmed by the sea of bitterness which enveloped me like a flood, and there seemed no way out. I just hated the killers and cursed them that they might suffer as I had suffered. I could see the fruit that resulted from so much anger, bitterness, rage, and hatred in my life. When this fruit took control, I was filled with misery. Instead of walking through the valley of the shadow of death, I was, in fact, burying myself deeper in a grave of bitterness and sadness. I was not aware of the powerful anger that took control of my life, and it began to eat me alive.

Now I can hardly believe how I embraced the fruit of anger in my life for so many years. My instinctive need for revenge led me into a trap of sinful desire. It corrupted my mind. The truth is, I failed to put on the new self with which my Shepherd intended for me to live. I needed to learn to let go of my natural instinctive need for revenge. I actually missed seeing the beauty of the new life in which my Shepherd wanted to lead me. He wanted to show me the joy of a relationship with Him. He wanted to show me the beauty of His healing grace for my journey with Him. Most of all, my Shepherd wanted to set me free from the bondage of my personal instincts so that I could worship Him and live joyfully. When I went to speak at a number of churches in Northern Ireland, a few people asked me, "Why did you take so long to let it go?"

I responded, "I must admit that I am not a perfect man. I am a broken man. It was not easy for me to let my anger go. The essence of my culture had taken deep root in my life. The pursuit of family honour took a deep root in my attitude. It took me a long time to learn to let it go. I needed time to learn to be transformed from the inside out. I needed to learn to change." I believe that many people mistakenly thought it was not so difficult to change.

I did not want to simply tell them what they wanted to hear. By this time, I wanted to be honest with people. I had my own struggles that I needed to work through. It was not an easy journey for me, but I learned through my struggle not to give up. It would take a long time to be transformed, but at least I kept moving, even though progress was slow.

As I journeyed with the Shepherd of my soul, I began to learn more about my Christian faith. I needed to be cleansed from bitterness, anger, disappointment, and hatred inside my heart. These negative emotions were stuck in my heart for years because I was unwilling to pull them out. Honestly, in my own strength, I could never get rid of these negative emotions. I needed to rely on the power of the grace of the Shepherd of my soul to uproot them from my heart. I had to learn to be transformed by the knowledge of my Shepherd. Transformation takes a lifetime. If I were to stop learning to change, I would be finished. I would become spiritually dead and likely fall into my old self.

I have been living in the Canadian culture long enough to learn that people expect quick results. They do not like the process of transformation, which is a slow process. I have observed this tendency in Western society. People are influenced by the instant or quick fix mentality—we want things done quickly. We have instant cash, instant noodles, instant coffee, instant delivery, fast food, fast internet, and so on.

Life transformation takes time. It takes time to cut out the deep-rooted sinful desires inside our hearts. We need time to dig deeper so that we can cut it all out. Change does not happen after hearing one preached message, or one counselling session, or reading the Bible one time and being changed the next day.

My sinful desire did not die in water baptism. It does not happen that way. It took me many years to learn to change. I wish I could learn to change quickly, but my old self did not die in baptism water. My new faith did not grow after I finished reading one round of the Bible. Spiritual growth takes time for me to learn to build up my faith in my Shepherd. It is a slow process to maturity.

I am grateful to my Shepherd for sparing my life from the grave. My enemies wanted me dead. They succeeded in killing my family, but my Shepherd spared my life from the grave. He has a special purpose for my life. I could never forget what I heard them say about me the night after I was brought back to the village, three days after my family was killed. They said, "If you dig the grass, you need to dig all its roots, otherwise it will come back." As soon as I heard this phrase, my heart sank. I felt as though my heart was being pierced by a sharp knife. I knew what it meant. It signified that if they were going to kill a family, they needed to kill all of its members—sparing no one. Otherwise, the survivors would come back to take revenge. What they said would never be erased from my brain. I tried so hard to live, to move on, in the hope that I could fulfill my first promise made in front of the grave. It was to take revenge for my family. My enemies wanted to dig all its roots out, but my Shepherd spared my life from their eradication. I longed to fulfill the first promise I made in front of the grave.

In my culture, as a man who had survived such a horror, revenge would be considered the only way to honour my family. Failing to take revenge would have meant that I brought disgrace to my family. It was hard to live with the failure to fulfill my first promise. It was not the only disgrace I had to go through. I went through hell after my family was killed. I suffered tremendous pain. I went through depression, flashbacks, nightmares, anxiety disorders, insomnia, loneliness, hopelessness, and more…

As I examined my relationship with the Shepherd of my soul, I realized that this was not healthy for me. My spiritual growth was limited by my natural instincts—the ways I wanted. I could not bring myself closer to this Shepherd, because my life was ruled by anger and bitterness. I failed to uproot it earlier and replace it with a healthy root. Paul pointed out, *"You used to walk in these ways, in the life you once lived. But now you must also rid yourselves of all such things as these: anger, rage, malice, slander, and filthy language from your lips"* (Colossians 3:7-8). As a result of failing to uproot my anger and bitterness earlier, it produced a lot of rotten roots which brought my life into a deep depression. It only brought cancer to my soul. My attitude was living with the pursuit of honour for my family. I came across this Scripture so many times, but I did not want to address my anger.

When I was at Tyndale University and Providence Seminary, I heard preachers, professors, and pastors preach a lot about anger and bitterness, but I did not bother to explore more about my own inner anger and bitterness. In addition, I had read many books dealing with anger, but they did not touch my heart. I had learned from my head, but there was no conviction in my heart. I think that inside my heart, I was paralyzed by my anger. I just kept it deep in my heart and suppressed it. I did not want to look at it. I did not know how to handle my anger and bitterness. The truth was, the head knowledge could never change my stubborn attitude of taking revenge.

My personal instinct deeply influenced my stubborn attitude. Even though I had been a Christian for almost ten years, I was still struggling inside my heart. I did not want to look at my unresolved anger and inside my negative attitude. I was just a young Christian. I needed time to journey through life. To put it in simple theological terms, I failed to put my anger and bitterness to death. My sin was alive. My old self had not died yet. I was living in the old way. I had not changed much yet. I allowed the root of anger and bitterness to take deep root in my heart.

My sinful anger caused my mind to think in a sinful way and this sinful anger became the attitude of my life. Proverbs 4:23 describes my attitude correctly, *"Above all else, guard your heart, for everything you do flows from it."* I failed to guard my heart from my anger, and it resulted in a sinful longing—revenge. This sinful desire became the attitude of my life for years. I knew that this was not healthy. I was not supposed to live with such sinful anger. What I actually wanted to do grew from my sinful desire.

I must honestly admit that I was born with both natural and sinful desires, and these natural desires are good when I use them in accordance with the boundary my Shepherd intends for my life. Things I want outside of my Shepherd's boundary and intention are born out of my sinful desires. Period. Wanting to take revenge was not my Shepherd's intention for my life, but it was born out of my sinful desire. There were tensions between my natural and sinful desires. I must admit that I was wrestling with these desires. My struggle was very simple when I turned away from my Shepherd's boundary. I drifted away from my Shepherd; I became blinded and helpless. I fell into darkness and depression.

It took many years of my Christian journey to learn to walk through what my Shepherd desires for my life. It was not an easy road for me. My desire from my flesh was very powerful in my life. My own way, my own pursuit of my family's honour, and my own unresolved grief took deep root in my life. Anything I did apart from my Shepherd's leading would cause me to fall into a trap of my sinful desires. I realized that I needed to use my natural desires in accordance with my Shepherd's boundary for my life, which involved getting rid of my sinful anger.

My Shepherd called me to get rid of all my sinful anger and replaced it with the beauty of His grace, not the pursuit of family honour. I needed to put the culture of revenge to death and replace it with the culture of love. The culture of revenge brought only cancer to my soul, which kept hindering my spiritual growth. My desire to know more about my Shepherd was interrupted by this deadly cancer. I could never imagine that anger and bitterness taking deep root in my heart for so long would become the cancer of my soul. I had struggled a lot with this anger and bitterness.

As a consequence, my spiritual growth deteriorated. What was the point of living with the cancer of my soul? I could not establish my relationship with the Shepherd of my soul. I could not draw closer to Him. I needed to recognize my sinful belief and replace it with what the Shepherd of my soul wanted me to live with.

I went to speak at a number of places in many different countries. Many people asked me some good questions regarding my anger and bitterness. One young man in Northern Ireland asked, "Tell me briefly why your anger and bitterness were hindering your relationship with the Lord."

I responded and said, "I wish I could offer you theories or ideas briefly that would help you. In fact, it is a long story for me to tell you."

I did mention earlier that I felt unworthy of joining the table with the Shepherd of my soul. There are many ways that anger can create relational problems. For me, personally, I strongly believe that my Shepherd calls me to be holy because He is holy. *"But just as he who called you is holy, so be holy in all you do; for it is written: Be holy, because I am holy"* (1 Peter 1:15-16).

As I examined this passage, I came to understand that my Shepherd calls me, a sinner, to learn to be transformed to be holy like Him. Therefore, I must learn to be holy in whatever I do, in conversation, thinking, and behaving towards all people—friends, or enemies. My personal responsibility as a Christian is to be holy because my Shepherd is holy. He has called me to imitate Him. He is perfectly, unchangeably, and eternally holy. To be holy should be a desire of my life.

Now, how could I be holy when my heart was filled with the cancer of my soul? How could I come closer to my Shepherd when inside, my heart was filled with the sinful anger? I had been struggling with this anger and bitterness for years. This unresolved anger and bitterness in my life brought dishonour and displeased my Shepherd. I failed in my personal responsibility to be holy.

My dear brothers and sisters, take note of this: Everyone should be quick to listen, slow to speak and slow to become angry, because human anger does not produce the righteousness that God desires (James 1:19-20).

It was true that my personal anger offended my Shepherd. I failed to live my life the way my Shepherd intended for me. This was an obvious reason why my spiritual growth was dragged down by my sinful anger and bitterness. My personal relationship with my Shepherd was blocked by my sinful anger. There was no room in my heart for my spiritual growth. My Shepherd intended for me to live a healthy life, but my inner turmoil was preventing that.

Inside my heart, I felt torn in two different directions. I was absolutely lost and confused. In my young Christian walk, my anger and bitterness pulled me down into a deep, dark side of life. My anger and bitterness had brought me no satisfaction; it had destroyed my health, my peace of mind, and my spiritual relationship with the Lord.

During the first few years of my Christian life, anger, bitterness, and depression ruled me. I had no taste of the abundant life, and I knew nothing about Christian joy. I had no good Christian friends I could count on. My personal relationship with my Shepherd was not genuinely intimate. I did not know Him personally. I went to church every Sunday with a heart full of anger and bitterness. I could not absorb the teaching of the church. I did not know what the messages meant to me. My anger and bitterness ruined my personal relationship with my Shepherd. My life was supposed to bring honour, praise, and pleasure to my Shepherd, but anger and bitterness crippled me. I became spiritually depressed. I fell short of what my Shepherd desired of me. My simple joy of Christian life was robbed by my unresolved anger. The sad part of my life was that I allowed my anger to ruin my life.

In your anger do not sin: Do not let the sun go down while you are still angry, and do not give the devil a foothold (Ephesians 4:26-27).

In my early journey as a young Christian, I came across this Scripture so many times, but I did not bother to examine it seriously. I did not pay much attention to it. In fact, I allowed the devil to stay in my heart for years. Failing to resolve my anger was one thing. Now, I was sidetracked by my Shepherd's enemy. It contradicted the purpose of my life—to be holy. I failed to bring honour and praise to my Shepherd.

So we make it our goal to please him, whether we are at home in the body or away from it (2 Corinthians 5:9).

Paul encouraged all believers to try their best to please the Lord. Yet there I was nurturing my Shepherd's enemy inside my heart. There was a spiritual conflict inside my heart. How could I grow spiritually? It was impossible. This was part of the reason my spiritual growth was starved. Not only did I suffer from mental depression, but I also suffered from spiritual depression.

Failing to resolve my inner anger affected me socially, as well in my life. I did not have many good friends. I was so lonely. I chose isolation. I could rarely find someone who could understand my anger. As I scrutinized the early years after I lost my family, I realized that no one wanted to be my friend because I was an angry man.

Once my friend challenged me, "Reaksa, why do you get angry so quickly without a good reason?"

I could not handle his question. I walked away from him. I could tell that with the unresolved anger boiling in my heart for years, when anything insignificant arose in me, it sent a signal to my tank of unresolved anger, and created a spark of anger quickly. I did not need to have a logical reason to become angry. Any small, insignificant thing triggered my tank of unresolved anger, and it exploded quickly. How could I live in such a way?

For about six years after my family was killed, my life was filled with anger. My anger was associated with my desire to take revenge for my family. I lived daily with the fantasy of killing my enemies the way they had killed my family. I was totally lost within my own world of anger.

Later, I escaped to Thailand and went to live in Khao-I-Dang refugee camp. I carried my anger with me for many years. Eventually, I came to Canada in 1989. A year after that, I received Jesus Christ as my Lord and my Saviour. But the anger inside my heart did not subside. My anger became the attitude of my life. I unconsciously carried this negative attitude with me, even though I had become a Christian. Studying in the Christian schools, my anger still did not wane. I became very isolated. I hardly had any friends. The anger inside me kept me from having good relationships. I was very much alone.

Interestingly, I took my personality test three times through the "Personality Test of Myers & Briggs' 16 Types." It showed that I was very extroverted. But in reality, I was very much alone. Most of the time, I stayed in my room reading books, or I went to the local library to read. No one wanted to be my friend because I was an angry man. The book of wisdom from King Solomon pinpointed the infection of the attitude of my life in an accurate way,

Do not make friends with a hot-tempered person, do not associate with one easily angered, or you may learn their ways and get yourself ensnared (Proverbs 22:24-25).

This Scripture hit me like a huge earthquake. It was the best diagnosis of my attitude. I realized that the anger inside me not only hurt others, but it mostly hurt me. I needed to crawl out of this grave of anger.

The anger in my heart became the cancer of my soul. Life was not worth living with such cancer in my soul. This cancer took deep root in my life for a long time and it ate my personal conscience. It hindered my personal relationship

225

with the Shepherd of my soul. It never allowed me to feel thirsty for more of my Shepherd. I failed to live my life as my Shepherd intended for me. The worst scenario was that I was sidetracked and controlled by my Shepherd's enemy. Anger also hurt my relationship with others.

Paul encouraged, *"If it is possible, as far as it depends on you, live at peace with everyone"* (Romans 12:18). I did not know how to live at peace with others. I did not have many good friends. A few years after I graduated from Providence Seminary, I came to my final conviction that I needed to try my best to deal with my sinful anger, because my Shepherd had commanded me to do so. I was responsible for putting my sinful anger to death. I had to arise from my grave of anger. My personal instinct had to be put to death.

> *Therefore, brothers and sisters, we have an obligation— but it is not to the flesh, to live according to it. For if you live according to the flesh, you will die; but if by the Spirit you put to death the misdeeds of the body, you will live* (Romans 8:12-13).

If I did not put this cancer of the soul to death, it would destroy my life. *"A heart at peace gives life to the body, but envy rots the bones"* (Proverbs 14:30). I could no longer see the point of living with the cancer of my soul. This prayer of David helped me:

> *Blessed is the one whose transgressions are forgiven,*
> *whose sins are covered.*
> *Blessed is the one*
> *whose sin the Lord does not count against them*
> *and in whose spirit is no deceit.*

When I kept silent, my bones wasted away
through my groaning all day long.
For day and night, your hand was heavy on me;
my strength was sapped as in the heat of summer.
Then I acknowledged my sin to you
and did not cover up my iniquity.
I said, 'I will confess my transgressions to the Lord.'
And you forgave the guilt of my sin.
Therefore let all the faithful pray to you
while you may be found;
surely the rising of the mighty waters will not reach them.
You are my hiding place;
you will protect me from trouble and surround me
with songs of deliverance.

(Psalm 32:1-7)

PRAYER:

Lord, Shepherd of my soul, You are my Stronghold, my Salvation, and my Deliverer. Please have mercy on me. Please clean the sinful anger in my heart. Wash away all my anger and cleanse me from my sin. Lord, please deliver me from my sinful heart. I know my sin eats away my conscience. It hurts me the most. I do not want to live with my old self. Please renew a right spirit within me. Help me to be transformed into a new person.

Shepherd of my soul, please forgive me for allowing anger to take deep root in my heart. It destroys my personal relationship with You. My anger inside me makes it hard for me to come closer to You. I am not thirsty for You. The bitter root of anger got stuck inside my heart for too long. This root of anger has produced only rotten fruit in my life and it is not healthy for me.

Shepherd of my soul, please grant me the spiritual power to pull out the root of anger in my life and fill my heart with joy. Shepherd of my soul, I need Your grace and mercy to pull out this root of anger from my heart and replace it with a clean heart. I need to replace it with healthy fruit to help me produce more good fruit.

Shepherd of my soul, please grant me peace and cleanse my heart. Please fill me with an attitude of calmness and gentleness. Please set me free from this entangling anger. I need to move on with a healthy and positive conscience. Shepherd of my soul, deliver me from my sin and cleanse my heart as I move on in my journey, as I depend on Your grace. Amen.

THE SECOND PART OF THIS REFLECTION IS IN THE PRESENCE OF MY ENEMIES (PSALM 23:5)

Facing my enemies (those involved in killing my family) was the most difficult part for me. There were six people involved in killing my family. I found out that there were only two killers still surviving—one man who killed my father and another who killed my mother. My anger was born out of the motive of taking revenge for my family. With that resolving now, the Shepherd of my soul called me to another level in my journey with Him. It was a psychological revolution against life's unfairness. I needed to set myself free from the bondage of anger and bitterness by direct action. I needed to face my enemies and forgive them. It was the most difficult thing I have ever done.

I had done a lot of reading on PTSD. I found a lot of scientific literature suggesting that forgiveness could bring healing. I thought that it would be good for me to learn about forgiving my family's killers. I never actually thought I could do it. As a Christian, I had learned a lot about forgiveness, but to put it into practice was a whole other matter. I could *say* I forgive my enemies from a distance, from Canada to Cambodia, but in reality, going "face to face" by making a trip to see them and forgive them was another extraordinary step in my life. The essence of forgiveness is a high moral calling for me to learn to imitate my Shepherd's example.

Learning the concept of forgiveness from schools, churches, and books was not hard for me. I could understand the essence of forgiveness. However, to actually live it out was a matter of flesh and blood. It was not naturally easy. I am a human being. I am not a robot. I felt hurt and uneasy about forgiving. I had lots of friends at schools and churches who knew some parts of my tragic story from the Killing Fields. They made some good suggestions about forgiveness. In counselling programs, I learned many theories about forgiveness. "Forgiveness brings healing." In churches, I heard many pastors preach a lot of good sermons about forgiveness. It sounded too good to be true. In Canada, people like to say, "The school of teaching is easier than the school of practice." In other words, "Easier said than done."

During the course of my twenty-year ministry in Cambodia, I met a good friend named Pak Soon Lau. Later, he became my ministry partner. He and I spent a lot of time travelling to visit many villages in Cambodia together. We had done a lot things together in the village where my family was killed. We learned a lot of things together. Once he wrote to me and told me honestly how hard it was to forgive. I was drawn by his honesty regarding the school of preaching versus the school of practicing. Here is what he wrote:

Dear Reaksa,

When I first read your life story, I felt sad and angry. I was sad to read of the evil done to you and your family and I was angry that the wicked seem to triumph. Yet towards the end of this narrative, you shared about the peace and freedom God granted to you to forgive these evil men. I was very touched— both by your willingness to forgive and your honest admission of your struggle to forgive. But most of all, I was overwhelmed by the incredible miracle that God has wrought in your heart.

However, all these emotions and thoughts remained outside the realm of my personal life. They were real, no doubt, but yet far from the reality of my day-to-day existence.

Then God granted me this tremendous privilege of working with you in partnership to serve him in Cambodia. Suddenly the words, the thoughts, and the emotions took on flesh and bones. Working with you, hearing you share about your plans to bless the Cambodians, and watching you minister to a people that once hurt you so deeply, has made me feel ashamed of my own inability to forgive.

It has not been easy working by your side. Why? Because your life exposed the great gulf between beliefs and practice that existed in my own life. I asked myself, "Would I be able to forgive the killers of my entire family?" I found myself weak and lacking in this area.

Somebody once said, "The weak can never forgive. Forgiveness is the attitude of the strong." Reaksa, you are the strong one and I thank God for the strength He has put in you. Surely it takes divine love and strength to not only forgive, but also to seek to meet the killers, one by one, so that you could tell them face-to-face that you forgive them and to bless them with gifts.

Truly this is repaying evil with good. Truly this is the gospel of Jesus Christ clothed with flesh and blood! It is my prayer that the Lord will continue to use you to proclaim the message of forgiveness and reconciliation—a message that the world needs to hear and the church needs to recover. May the Lord bless you richly.

Your friend, Pak Soon Lau

As a pastor and a missionary, he was very careful with his words. He was very honest with me. I really appreciated the way he acknowledged that he found himself weak and lacking in areas of forgiveness. In fact, I also inserted this letter in my second book, *After the Heavy Rain*. I am using it again in this book because I do not want to send the wrong message to people who think that forgiveness is easy. It is hard to learn to forgive. There is no shortcut to forgiveness. There is no magical solution that helps me to forgive quickly. I had to go through a long, painful journey. My late father used to tell me, "Don't tell people to do something you do not want to do, and don't tell people to do things you never did." This is wisdom from my late father.

In the process of writing this chapter, I got an email from a wonderful young lady. She wrote:

Dear Reaksa,

I was wondering if I could ask you a few questions about your book, *Tears of My Soul*. Did you find it hard? How long did it take for you to *fully* forgive? After facing traumatic events, how did it change you as a man, a dad, and a husband?

My family has gone through a lot of traumas as well, and I lost my dad at a young age, very young. Then we got sent to a refugee camp, got here, and everything was new, and my sister and I were sexually abused by our grandfather, and another man sexually abused her.

To this day, I find it awfully painful to even hear about them and I am the type of person to hold grudges. It must have been very hard for you because what you went through does not compare to mine at all. If you have time, please call me.

Sincerely yours,
Mary (not her real name)

She gave me her number. I decided to give her a call. She was so excited as soon as she heard my name. She said, "I started reading your book, and I could not put it down. That is why I decided to write to you to ask you these few questions." I had a pleasant conversation with her. At first, she was expecting me to give her a quick formula to forgive those who hurt her and her sister. I told her that I wished I could help her with a formula to forgive, but I had none. There was no such quick formula to forgive. I could hear her disappointment. In our conversation, she realized that it was very hard for her to forgive. She wanted to let it go, but she did not know how to forgive. It was very painful for her to talk about all her tragic experiences. She asked me to make a few suggestions.

I said, "Mary, you have a choice to forgive your enemy. It is not easy, but you have a choice to make. You have the liberty to choose to set yourself free from people who hurt you. It is a psychological revolution against your life's unfairness and injustice. The only way to move on in your journey is to set yourself free from the bondage of bitterness. If not, you will become a prisoner to the pain and bitterness in your life. You may not be able to do this difficult task alone. You may need someone who can help you to go through the process of suffering. You may need to have people pray for you."

All I could hear from her was, "It is very difficult. I do not know how to bring myself to forgive." It is true that forgiveness is very difficult.

I could sense that Mary had gone through a hard time learning to forgive. It was hard for her to make the decision to forgive. She was trying to justify what had happened with her family. As I listened to her, I could relate to her problems. I once was struggling with my self-justification—"I am right and they are wrong"—mental attitude. With this attitude, it was hard for me to forgive. My self-justification led me into the bondage of bitterness and depression.

Consciously, I was trying to justify my anger. It was not fair for my family. My family's killers deserved death at my hand. My mind was wrongfully programmed towards taking revenge. Nothing else had significance in my life except pursuing honour for my family by taking revenge. This was the top priority in my life, and I tried to define my own justice and my own law. I could not forgive because the pain and hurt was so deep. If I did not take vengeance, I would feel guilty about not honouring my family. The pain and hurt in my heart scolded me day after day, telling me that I was not a big man, and I had failed my family. I could not forgive because my life was turned upside down by my family's killers. I could never be the same again because it had transformed my existence into darkness. My life's happiness was stolen from me. My normal thinking was disrupted by restless thoughts and confused feelings.

Forgiveness is not easy. I have received many emails from those who read my second book. They wrote to me they had a hard time forgiving their offenders. They tried to tell me the one-sided stories about their self-justifications. They were right and their offenders were wrong. They could not forgive their offenders. One man wrote, after many exchanged emails with me in which he tried to justify his case, "But I know that's not what God wants of me. Like you, I am a Christian, but I struggle with this bitterness I nurtured every day. Not a day passes by in which I don't fantasize about killing everyone and myself and watch them get tortured in hell. How could I forgive? They were absolutely wrong." I could absolutely relate to his experience. I tried for years to justify my case. It was not worth living with such self-justification. It brought nothing, except unresolved anger and depression.

Many years after I had lost my family, I was still living in bitterness. I felt as though my life was still overwhelmed by the sea of bitterness which enveloped me like a flood, and there seemed no way out! I became emotionally crippled and I did not know how to deal with it. I just hated the killers and cursed them that they might suffer as I did. Finally, I longed to hear my family's killers admit that what they had done was wrong. I wanted to hear them say that they were sorry. I realized that forgiveness was hard, but my self-justification led me into deep, dark depression.

It is easy to teach about forgiveness, but it is not easy to practice it. I remembered one story from a pastor. He told a story like this:

"There was a pastor in a church. He was preaching about forgiveness to a big congregation. It happened that his mother-in-law came to hear him preach about forgiveness and she sat near the pastor's wife. When he was preaching about forgiveness, he was making a lot of good points about forgiveness.

"His wife just kept raising her hand. 'Yes! That is correct. Hallelujah, praise the Lord.' From the start to the end of his preaching, his wife kept raising her hand and shouting "Hallelujah! Hallelujah!" At the end of his sermon, the pastor's mother-in-law turned to her daughter and said, 'Your husband preached very well about forgiveness.' Her daughter was so stunned, but she responded, 'Yes, he always preaches well at the church, but he does not practice it at home.'"

I spent a few years reflecting on the full meaning of Psalm 23:5. I tried to make sense of it in my own context. As far as it depends on me, I needed to live at peace with my enemies. How was that possible? It would be impossible if it depended on my own power. However, it was possible if I depended on the grace of my Shepherd. I did not want to take revenge anymore. I decided to cancel what I actually wanted to do many years before. I needed to learn to forgive. I was called to reverse my own personal psychological revolution against life's injustices. I was no longer living in the bondage of my old self, but I was a new person in the Shepherd of my soul. I was called to be His ambassador. My life should reflect me as a new person in my Shepherd. My responsibility, as an ambassador of my Shepherd, is to invite my enemies to join the feast of honour with my Shepherd. I had to forgive my enemies and be reconciled with them as much as it was reasonably possible. Paul beautifully puts it this way:

> *Therefore, if anyone is in Christ, the new creation has come: The old has gone, the new is here! All this is from God, who reconciled us to himself through Christ and gave us the ministry of reconciliation: that God was reconciling the world to himself in Christ, not counting people's sins against them. And he has committed to us the message of reconciliation. We are therefore Christ's ambassadors, as though God were making his appeal through us. We implore you on Christ's behalf: Be reconciled to God. God made him who had no sin to be sin for us so that in him we might become the righteousness of God* (2 Corinthians 5:17-21).

My Shepherd, who is holy and sinless, prepared the table for me. He generously invited me to join the feast of honour with Him. He did not count my countless sins, but He graciously accepted me at His table. He did not look at my sins and exclude me from His invitation. I had learned that my Shepherd, who is the sinless Son of God, had come into this broken world in order to reconcile the world to Himself. He had put Himself in the position of being actually reconciled to me as a sinner. Now, He wanted me to invite my enemies to share the table too. He wanted me to return to meet my enemies, to forgive them, and to be reconciled with them. I would never have imagined that I could do this, but His Spirit dwells in me.

My Shepherd had spared my life from the grave and given me the ministry of forgiveness and reconciliation with my enemies. I knew that this ministry of forgiveness and reconciliation would never make sense to the people there, but it was very important for me as a Christian. They had been living in a primitive culture. They had never heard the name of my Shepherd. Actually, there was no such Christian teaching of forgiveness and reconciliation in this community. I imagined doing this, but I could not even imagine how they would respond to my forgiveness. Would they accept my forgiveness? There were more questions in my mind than answers.

In June 2003, more than twenty years after my family was killed, I decided to return to the village to express my forgiveness to the two surviving killer families. I went there to proclaim the living testimony of the grace of my Shepherd in my life. I needed to put the things I had learned about forgiveness into practice. It required strong emotional energy and personal determination to accomplish this almost impossible mission. It had to come from my pure and sincere heart. Even though I was ready to undertake this mission, I knew that I would be hurt again. But for the sake of my own healing, I had to bear the hurt and endure the second pain so that my soul, once drenched in agony and despair beyond words, would be fully restored to real life in my Shepherd.

I spent a lot of time praying for my trip to forgive my enemies. I knew that I could not do this in my own strength. I needed emotional and psychological support. I decided to take two young men I had mentored to be pastors for the community to go with me. For me, making such a trip to forgive my enemies meant that I was willing to accept the second level of emotional pain and hurt, but I strongly believed that it would set me free. I honestly told the two young men that I desperately needed their company, their emotional, prayer, and moral support. They did not comprehend what I was about to do. One of the men was very shy and quiet.

On the way to the village, he said, "If I were you, I would not know what to do, and I would not have the guts to face those who had murdered my family. It is too difficult, and a painful decision, but I am very proud of you." I was encouraged by his few words. He did not realize that inside my heart I was struggling. He might have thought that I was strong, but the truth was that I felt weak, and unsure as to how I could face my enemies. I kept reciting my prayer that my Shepherd would grant me the strength to be able to accomplish this "mission impossible." I kept encouraging myself with this verse:

I can do all this through him who gives me strength (Philippians 4:13).

I finally learned to surrender my life to my Shepherd to lead me to forgive my enemies. It was a painful journey to learn to surrender, but it was the best journey to set myself free from the bondage of anger, bitterness, and pain.

About a mile from the village, I could feel the sharpness of painful memories intensifying in my heart. My heart started to pound faster and faster. My lips began to freeze and my face became red. Inside my heart, I was filled with mixed emotions—fear, sadness, anger, and pain. I was torn between my own instinct and my Shepherd's teaching. I was struggling with my flesh. I could tell that my nervousness started to kick at my soul. I decided to stop and pray:

"Lord, Shepherd of my soul, I feel uneasy approaching this village. The unwanted emotions are stirring within me. Please help me handle these in a healthy way and with a Christian character that reflects Yours. I need Your guidance. Lord, please protect my anger inside me. Help me to show a proper manner of forgiveness that reflects Your character.

"My Shepherd, I need to be a good ambassador. I come back to this village to invite my enemies to join the feast of honour with You. I will offer them forgiveness. Please show me grace, courage, and strength to face them. It is very painful for me. Have mercy upon me and renew my heart as I forgive my enemies. I am a human being. I feel hurt and pained, but I know that You are going with me. Please help me accomplish this almost impossible mission of forgiveness.

"My Shepherd, such forgiveness is proof of Your greatness and Your love in my life. Now I need to show this great love to my enemies. It may never make sense to them, but it will bring healing for my heart and soul.

"O my Shepherd, I want to release all my unresolved anger, bitterness, hatred, and pain from my heart. Please help me do what is right and help me know what to say to them. I know that it will be difficult, but help me not to rely on my own strength and wisdom. Please help me prevent my human instincts from rising up when I meet my enemies. Instead, I shall rely on your grace.

"Shepherd of my soul, this is the most important chapter of my life, to set myself free from the bondage of anger, bitterness, and pain. Shepherd of my soul, help me to accomplish my unfinished business here. I need a new start in life, so I am choosing to forgive my enemies by letting go of all the pain and hurt of the past, and I am choosing to receive healing for my wounds. I choose healing from my psychological trauma—PTSD.

"Shepherd of my soul, I know that You have spared my life and taken me back to this village for just this special purpose. Please help me rely on Your strength and grace. Help me to behave as Your ambassador. Be with me, O Shepherd of my soul. I need Your help. I need You to guide me to behave in an appropriate way, that will reflect your character of forgiveness and love. I pray and I entrust this trip into Your hands as I am going to enter the village now, in the name of Jesus Christ, the Shepherd of my soul. Amen."

After praying, I felt a little bit more peaceful, but my nervousness did not stop. I continued my trip to enter the village. I was reminded of what Paul said in Philippians 3:13-14:

Forgetting what is behind and straining toward what is ahead, I press on towards the goal to win the prize for which God has called me heavenward in Christ Jesus.

I could feel myself shaking, but I had to press on to meet my enemies.

Most of the people in the village were so surprised as soon as they heard my name. It had been so long ago. Now, I was back in the village looking for those involved in killing my family, to forgive them. At first, they did not believe me. They were so skeptical about us. In the culture of revenge, there was no such word as "forgiveness." Who would believe that we came back to meet my family's killers and offer forgiveness? Would it be possible? How? Our good intention was not accurately understood. In their minds, they thought that I had come to kill those men who killed my family more than twenty-five years ago. They had no idea what we were about to do. My two friends tried to explain my motive. It took them a little while to convince the villagers. I could perceive a mood shift in some of them, showing signs of acceptance. However, other people were still skeptical about my motives. It did not make sense to them. It was unthinkable that anyone would ever come to search for their enemies and forgive them.

Finally, I met one of the men who killed my father. I forgave him. I offered him a Cambodian scarf as a symbol of my forgiveness for him, a shirt as a symbol of my love for him, and a Bible as a symbol of my blessing for him. I read Luke 23:34:

"Father, forgive them for they do not know what they are doing."

I told him, "I have come here to forgive you." I read this passage aloud and declared "I forgive you." It gave me power over my enemy. I was no longer his prisoner. I had set myself free. Forgiveness is not easy to accomplish, but by the grace of my Shepherd, I had accomplished the most difficult mission in my life. After that, I gave him a hug. I hugged the man who killed my father. His body was shaking badly. I could tell that my enemy felt so frightened.

I told him, "Twenty-eight years ago, when you took me to the jungle, I was so terrified. But today, I came here as an ambassador of Jesus Christ. I set you free." He did not understand what I was saying to him. Forgiving my enemy was one thing, but giving him a hug was at another level. The moment I hugged him I could tell inside my heart that my twenty-odd years of anger that had been burning my heart had subsided. It was not a magic fix, but it was the grace of my Shepherd with me. The healing power of the Shepherd of my soul cooled down my long-standing anger. My Shepherd replaced my angry heart of stone with a loving heart of flesh. In hugging my enemy, one image came to my mind: my Shepherd on the Cross. Despite all the physical pain and psychological torture, He still called out to His heavenly Father, "Father, forgive them, for they know not what they are doing."

Regarding Ean, the man who killed my mother, I went to look for him three times. The first two times, I could not find him. Finally, I got to meet him. I decided to confront him:

Reaksa: "Thank you for giving me an opportunity to meet you today. In fact, I tried to look for you twice before, but I could not find you."

Ean: "I was told that you came to look for me twice, but I was not home. I knew that you wanted me to travel to meet you in the city, but I was afraid to meet you there. In fact, I did not know where to find you in the city. My wife did not want me to go there. She was so afraid that you would take revenge."

Reaksa: "Why was she afraid of me?"

Ean: "No one in the history of this village has come back to forgive the killers. They only come back to settle the old account."

Reaksa: "I am a Christian; I do not believe in killing. I believe in the love and forgiveness of Jesus Christ. If I were not a Christian, I would come back to settle the old account or I would send someone to settle the old account for me. My Lord teaches me to love, not hate, to forgive, not take revenge. We obey our Lord's teaching. The main theme in Christian teaching is love. It is through the love of the teaching of Jesus Christ that helps me to learn to forgive. It is His love that melts the hatred and bitterness in my soul. This is the main reason I come here to meet you to forgive you. I thank God that I can meet you today. I feel as though I have completed the most difficult mission in my life."

Ean: "Your God is so good. You are well educated and you come to forgive me. Can you tell me more about your God?"

Reaksa: "Of course, I will tell you about my God, but first let me ask you, how did you feel when you took my family to be executed in the jungle?"

Ean: "We were so afraid."

Reaksa: "But why did you and your associates cheer while killing the victims?"

Ean: "I did not know what I did on that day. I am so sorry. I felt as though some kind of dark spirit was controlling me. I thought that I was mad. When I started killing the first few people, I was so afraid, but after that I did not know why we cheered. We lost our humanity. We were like animals. Our madness made us so evil... I am so sorry."

As I looked at his face as he described what was happening on that day, and how he and his associates killed my family, I saw his remorse and regret for what he had done to my family. His confession of inhumanity indicated his genuine sincerity. He was so brave to tell me what actually happened. I realized that I had pressed him so

243

deep. It was painful to listen to what actually happened to my family. It triggered my emotions. I was reminded of what Paul said, *"Do not let any unwholesome talk come out of your mouths, but only what is helpful for building others up according to their needs, that it may benefit those who listen"* (Ephesians 4:29).

I realized that if I kept digging deeper and deeper into what happened to my family, I might lose my control or bad words might slip out of my mouth. It might trigger my anger, in which I might lose my patience and most of all, I might fail in my mission of forgiveness. I knew that I had come back to this village to be an ambassador of my Good Shepherd. What I needed to do is to show a true picture of the character of forgiveness of my Shepherd. I decided to stop digging for more questions from Ean. My purpose was to love my family's killers and forgive them. I came back to bring peace to my enemies, not to make war. My Good Shepherd said, *"Blessed are the peacemakers, for they will be called children of God"* (Matthew 5:9). I believed that my Shepherd was pleased with me bringing peace to my family's killers.

Finally, I said to Ean, "I would like to cancel whatever happened in the deepest, darkest history of my family. Let's begin a new thing together. I abolish all past painful history from my heart, and we will start again with a fresh journey. Allow me to assure you again. I come back to forgive you. Please tell your wife and family not to worry. I met her a few hours ago when I went to look for you at the Rok village, but you were not there. Your wife told me that you were here at this village. I decided to come to look for you here. I am glad that I met you here. She was so afraid that I would kill you. In fact, she begged me to spare your life. I assured her again and again that I came to forgive you."

Ean said, "I am so sorry. Please forgive me. Thank you so much for forgiving me."

I felt released after I heard him ask me to forgive him. In fact, I longed to hear these words for almost thirty years of my life. As I heard these words, I wept. My most difficult mission was accomplished. I had forgiven my family's killers. I could see the smile on his face. He accepted my forgiveness.

I said to Ean, "As I promised to tell you more about my God, please let me read a Scripture to you from John 3:16-18:

"For God so loved the world that he gave his one and only Son, that whoever believes in him shall not perish but have eternal life. For God did not send his Son into the world to condemn the world, but to save the world through him. Whoever believes in him is not condemned, but whoever does not believe stands condemned already because they have not believed in the name of God's one and only Son."

After I read these verses for him, he did not clearly understand. It was the first time in his life he had heard about Jesus. He had no clue at all. I slowly tried to explain to him what it meant. "If you open your heart to accept Jesus Christ as your Lord and Saviour, your sin is forgiven. My Lord will forgive you." He still did not understand.

Reaksa: "Let me ask you a question. If your hands get dirty, what do you clean your hands with?"

Ean: "I will use soap to clean my hands."

Reaksa: "That is correct. If you believe in Jesus, He will clean your sin by forgiving you. His precious blood will wash away your sin. Nothing else can take away your sin, except the precious blood of Jesus Christ."

He only smiled at me. He did not clearly understand what I was trying to explain to him. He needed more time to learn about Jesus.

I put a Cambodian scarf on his shoulder as a symbol of my forgiveness of him. I put my shirt on him as a symbol of my love for him. I gave him a Khmer Bible as a symbol of my blessing. Then, I gave him a hug and said, "Father, forgive him. He did not know what he did to my family."

I drew on every ounce of courage to repeat these words to my enemies. Many villagers were happy to see me hugging my enemies. It was a bit uncultural for a man to hug another man. My hope was that they had recorded, in their hearts, evidence of Christian forgiveness in this village. Tears kept rolling down my face. I had done the most difficult mission my Shepherd had called me to do. I imagined Him looking down at me from heaven saying, "Well done, my obedient sheep! Bravo, my sheep, you have been set free indeed."

My two friends who accompanied me were speechless. One of them came behind me and put his hand on my shoulder. It was a sign of acceptance and appreciation. After forgiving the man who killed my father, I had my lunch with him. I brought bread from the city and shared it with him. I celebrated with my enemy. It was a joyful celebration with him. Sitting down in front of my enemy watching him eat my bread, I could not understand his feelings. I was not so sure what he was thinking in his mind, but I could tell that he accepted my forgiveness. After I forgave him, I heard him say, "Thank you." He did not know what else to say to me. I think that he was in a state of shock. He could not understand my best intention for him. I broke bread (French baguette) in half and gave half to him. He extended his two hands to receive the bread from me (it is a sign of respect to receive the bread with two hands). I was contemplating on his two hands swinging a hoe on the heads of the members of my family. Actually, these two hands swung the hoe on my neck. Now, these two hands received the bread from me. What a contrast!

Many people were watching us sitting on the wooden floor eating together in a circle and they were talking about me when I was a young boy in the village. I did not pay much attention to what they were saying, but I was contemplating how my Shepherd had led my journey from the deep, dark valley of my life to the point of forgiving my enemy. My Shepherd's guidance was unfathomable. It was the most memorable celebration with the man who killed my father.

Twenty-eight years ago, a moment after I disentangled myself from the dead bodies over me, in my high peak of rage, I was strongly determined to take revenge for my family. Now, I had forgiven my enemy and had lunch with him. Nothing is impossible with my Shepherd. I never would have imagined that I could do this. I would never dream that it would be possible for me. What I actually wanted to do, I could not do. I did what I never wanted to do. I broke the first promise I made in front of the grave of my family. My Shepherd changed my heart. I cut out my bitter heart—a heart full of vengeance—and replaced it with a heart of love. My Shepherd came to die for me on the Cross and because of His love, He came to pay for my sin. Nothing else is more important than the heart of love from my Shepherd. My

Shepherd transformed my bitter heart to a heart of love and forgiveness. Now, I needed to show the transparency of this heart of love to my enemies.

As I decided to forgive my enemy, I kept guarding my heart to not fall into the trap of fulfilling my first promise of taking revenge. I strongly focused on my mission—I must forgive my enemy. Proverbs 4:23 clearly indicates the attitude of my heart, *"Above all else, guard your heart, for everything you do flows from it."* My attitude, decision, and choice of choosing to forgive my enemy was flowing from my pure heart. A new heart my Shepherd gave me—a heart of love and forgiveness.

I had to forgive because I needed to start a new life. My body was not built to carry negative emotions. The road to emotional healing was not always easy. It demanded all my emotional energy to rely on the grace of my Shepherd to cut down all negative feelings. I had had enough bitterness in my life and needed to move on, because my Shepherd had given me a new purpose. I could no longer allow myself to be infected by the cancer of my soul, or it would destroy me. Life should be a joyful journey with my Shepherd. I had to forgive because I needed to live my life to glorify my beloved Saviour and Shepherd. Building up a solid relationship with my Shepherd is the most vital journey for me.

My Shepherd said,

> *"Love the Lord your God with all your heart*
> *and with all your soul*
> *and with all your mind.*
> *This is the first and greatest commandment."*

(Matthew 22:37-38)

To love my Shepherd with great joy, I needed to uproot all my bitterness. I believe that my Shepherd smiled at me when I forgave my enemies. He had shown me on the Cross how He had set me free from sins by forgiving me. I received this gift of forgiveness freely, and I needed to transfer this gift of forgiveness to my enemies freely also. I had to imitate my Shepherd's great example. His gift of forgiveness on the Cross demands an act of obedience from me. I often recited this in my prayer, "*Forgive us our debts, as we also have forgiven our debtors*" (Matthew 6:12).

My act of forgiveness reflected my obedience to my Shepherd, and it reflected the demonstration of my Shepherd's love to my enemies. The message of loving our enemies is the most fundamental in His teaching.

> *[He said,] "Love your enemies,*
> *do good to those who hate you,*
> *bless those who curse you,*
> *pray for those who mistreat you."*

(Luke 6:27-28)

I chose to start over again and I chose to cancel what I actually wanted to do to them many years ago. I chose to stop pursuing honour for my family. I chose to replace hate with love. I chose to learn to love my family's killers. I chose healing for the wounds I had endured for many years.

The good news is that by the grace of my Shepherd, everything is possible. Indeed, by loving my enemies I can be set free from the pain of my past; forgiveness gives me the freedom to move on. The message of love for my enemies transforms my life—from being paralyzed by the power of hatred to being free in the power of the Shepherd of my soul. I am a new person! Since my Shepherd loves me, I can pass on that love to my enemies.

Forgiveness is not to gain back what was initially lost, but to live with the loss by relying on the grace of my Shepherd to overcome the hurt and pain in life. For me, to forgive my enemies is to be set free from emotional bondage. It helps in releasing the power of the effects of traumatic events in my life. It sets me free from symptoms of PTSD such as nightmares, flashbacks, anger, hurt, depression, bitterness, and disappointment.

Prayer for releasing all of the symptoms of PTSD is the most vital for my healing journey. It is very hard to explain from a scientific perspective how prayer heals symptoms of PTSD. However, forgiveness releases all the unresolved griefs in my life. I never forgot what was done to my family, but by the grace of my Shepherd, I chose to forgive. From a psychological perspective, I can conclude that forgiveness puts me in the position to set me free from the bondage of anger and bitterness. It shifts me from powerlessness to power—I am stronger than my enemies. It is a psychological revolution against life's unfairness in my life. If my Shepherd sets me free, I shall be free indeed. From my personal spiritual experiences, I can conclude that prayers can certainly heal!

> *"If my people, who are called by my name,*
> *will humble themselves and pray*
> *and seek my face and turn from their wicked ways,*
> *then I will hear from heaven,*
> *and I will forgive their sin and will heal their land."*

(2 Chronicles 7:14)

Is anyone among you in trouble? Let them pray. Is anyone happy? Let them sing songs of praise. Is anyone among you sick? Let them call the elders of the church to pray over them and anoint them with oil in the name of the Lord. And the prayer offered in faith will make the sick person well; the Lord will raise them up. If they have sinned, they will be forgiven. Therefore confess your sins to each other and pray for each other so that you may be healed. The prayer of a righteous person is powerful and effective.

(James 5:13-16)

Forgiveness also helps me to establish my relationship with the Shepherd of my soul. Before I was able to forgive, I had had no joy in worshipping my Shepherd. I felt as though the anger and bitterness had robbed me of this joy. When bitterness had seeped into my bones, there was no joy in my life. How could I worship the Shepherd of my soul with joy when my life was crippled by bitterness?

The first and greatest commandment that my Shepherd gave is:

"Love the LORD your God with all your heart and with all your soul and with all your mind and with all your strength" (Mark 12:30).

For years I struggled with my bitterness and anger. How could I love my Shepherd when my heart was poisoned with these things? It was impossible to love my Shepherd with bitterness. The bitterness and anger ruled my heart because I could not forgive.

Now, I have removed the root of bitterness and anger so that I can freely glorify my Shepherd in my life. I

251

believe my Shepherd smiled at me when I forgave my enemies. I could invite my enemies to join the feast of honour
in front of my Shepherd. Years later, I could see the grace
of my Shepherd in my life. I knew that forgiveness was the
spiritual power that broke the chains that tied me up from
worshipping my Shepherd joyfully. It quenched the fire of
bitterness and dug out the roots of anger. I have been
released from the emotional bondage that had bound and
hampered me for years. This emotional bondage was
broken from me. I am free indeed. If the Shepherd of my
Soul sets me free, I am free indeed. I could see the beauty
of my journey in a positive way.

It was an incredible journey my Shepherd led me on. I
could never imagine how my Shepherd led me from the
grave to Canada, then back to the village to meet my enemies and forgive them. I chose to forgive my enemies
because I realized that I could never live with the root of
unforgiveness. That would have prevented me from wor-
shiping my Shepherd joyfully.

PRAYER:

Lord, Shepherd of my soul, You are my Rock of my salvation, my Defender. I am grateful You spared my life from the pit. Thank You for choosing me from the pit, and thank You for leading me from the pit to Canada and eventually bringing me back to meet my enemies and helping me to forgive them. It was an incredible journey You have led me on. In my own strength, I could never have made it. Thank You for guiding me from the deep, dark valley of my life to freedom. Thank You for preparing me for a feast of honour. Shepherd of my soul, thank You for renewing my spirit. Please continue to guide me to walk in the path of Your righteousness. Amen.

I would like to conclude with a song of thanksgiving from Psalm 100:1-5:

Shout for joy to the LORD, all the earth.
Worship the LORD with gladness;
come before him with joyful songs.
Know that the LORD is God.
It is he who made us, and we are his;
we are his people, the sheep of his pasture.
Enter his gates with thanksgiving
and his courts with praise;
give thanks to him and praise his name.
For the LORD is good
and his love endures forever;
his faithfulness continues
through all generations.

Your Review & Reflection

1. Take a few minutes to examine your heart. Is there any anger or bitterness? What should you do with it?

2. What do you want your Shepherd to create in you? How?

3. Who is your real enemy or enemies?

4. How do you face him/her/them?

5. Do you ever want to be reconciled with your enemy?

6. Is there anyone in your life whom you have not for-given?

7. What might it look like for God to "prepare a table" for you to forgive this person?

8. Write your prayers below:

6

MY SHEPHERD BLESSES MY LIFE

A call to bless others

Surely your goodness and love
will follow me all the days of my life,
and I will dwell
in the house of the Lord forever.

(Psalm 23:6)

The Lord not only protects David but also blesses him for the rest of his life. It is a wonderful journey for him. He acknowledges that his Shepherd blesses him and loves him all the days of his life. Nothing could separate him from the love of his Shepherd. He will remain in the house of his Shepherd forever. For David, as long as he lives, the most important part of his life is to worship his Shepherd. The Lord is his Shepherd. He wants nothing else, except to remain in the house of the Lord and praise Him. It is his joyful celebration. David anticipated that when he departed from this world, he would remain with his heavenly Father forever.

MY PERSONAL MEDITATION

My Good Shepherd blessed me

This is the last part of my meditation based on Psalm 23. Finding a quiet place to relax is helpful for meditation. I would recite in my mind, "Shepherd of my soul, thank You so much for Your goodness and love, and thank You for blessing me." To sit down to acknowledge my gratitude to the Shepherd of my soul was not as difficult as walking through the deep, dark valley. I think that the last part of this meditation is easy and peaceful. To close my eyes and paint a picture of myself sitting down in front of my Shepherd, giving thanks with my grateful heart was easy. I felt safe and secure in front of the Shepherd of my soul.

I look back to the past painful experience. I can only praise the Shepherd of my soul for delivering me from the Killing Fields. No way could I have survived without the Mighty hand of my Shepherd on me. My foster father had correctly concluded that my Shepherd chose me before I even knew Him. When I went to visit the graves of my family, I tried to remember how it appeared at that time. I could never have imagined I would survive.

I couldn't see my Shepherd's redemption in my life until I returned to visit the graves and looked back to the journey through the deep, dark valley. I began to realize that my Shepherd had been working through my life since I was knocked into the pit. His supreme power was on my life when I was in the pit. He prompted the killers not to bury the grave after the first round of killing. As I stood on the gravesite when I went to visit, one phrase that echoed in my mind was when one of the killers said, "Don't bury it yet. Some more enemies need to be finished in this grave." The killers did not close the grave. The bird was the sure sign of a miracle in my life. My Shepherd sent the bird to call me out of the grave. If I had stayed a little bit longer in the grave, I would have been executed there. If I had gone to the west side of the grave, I would've encountered my family's killers while they were dragging my mother, sister, and other women to be executed in the grave.

I went to visit the old watermelon farm and looked at the bamboo bush where I'd hidden. I could not see any reason the killers had not seen me, but that my Shepherd had blinded them. I could only acknowledge that the Shepherd of my soul had spared my life for a special purpose. Psalm 59:1-2 says:

> *Deliver me from my enemies, O God; be my fortress against those who are attacking me. Deliver me from evildoers and save me from those who are after my blood.*

My Shepherd took me out of the pit. He protected me from being seen by my enemies. They chased after me, but they could not find me. They could not even see me! My Shepherd had blinded them. He saved my life from the grave. He spared my life. Praise the Shepherd of my soul, for His love lasts forever. Psalm 118:28-29 says:

> *You are my God, and I will praise you;*
> *you are my God, and I will exalt you.*
> *Give thanks to the Lord, for he is good;*
> *his love endures forever.*

I give thanks to the Shepherd of my soul for delivering me from the deep, dark depression. It was a long, painful journey for me. Yet in my deep, dark valley my Shepherd was teaching me to trust Him, count on Him, and believe in Him, that He would set me free. Praise the Shepherd of my soul, I am no longer troubled by nightmares and flashbacks. I am set free from them. *"If the Son sets you free, you shall be free indeed"* (John 8:36). I am grateful that my Shepherd has set me free.

I wrote in my heart after I got out of the water of baptism, that no matter what difficulties I might face, I would continue to worship my Shepherd for the rest of my life. I would not turn back. I am grateful to the Shepherd of my soul that He has healed my brokenness and restored me. He gave me a new purpose in life.

PRAYER:

Lord, Shepherd of my soul, my Protector and Defender, I give thanks for what You have done for my life. You spared me from the grave. Thank You for blinding my enemies. You took me on a long journey from the deep, dark valley of my fears, depression, flashbacks, and nightmares. Shepherd of my soul, without Your love and mercy on my life, I would never be where I am now. You have blessed me abundantly. You have healed my broken soul. I am now whole again. Thank You, Jesus Christ, the Shepherd of my soul. Amen.

I would like to point to a Psalm of praise from David:

My heart, O God, is steadfast;
I will sing and make music with all my soul.
Awake, harp, and lyre!

I will awaken the dawn.
I will praise you, Lord, among the nations;
I will sing of you among the peoples.
For great is your love, higher than the heavens;
Your faithfulness reaches to the skies.
Be exalted, O God, above the heavens;
Let your glory be over all the earth.

(Psalm 108:1-5).

MY PERSONAL REFLECTION

My Shepherd called me to bless others

The Lord is my Shepherd; nothing else is important for me. As I look back to the moment when I was in the grave, I am grateful that my Shepherd spared my life. He chose me when I didn't even know Him. I was a broken teenage boy who was lost, hopeless, and depressed. He took me on a long journey through the Cambodian jungle, filled with landmines, to Thailand. Eventually He took me to Canada.

I found the Shepherd of my soul while in Canada. He restored my health, gave me an education, and a new family. He guided me back to meet my enemies and forgive them. It has been a tremendous journey for my life—the journey that defined who I am in Him. What else is more important than having the Shepherd of my soul?

From now on, worshipping and praising my Shepherd should be my top priority. I know, by faith, when I leave this departure lounge, I will be in the house of my Shepherd in heaven where there are many mansions; there is nothing else I need.

My Shepherd has abundantly blessed me. He has guided me to meet many good people around the world. I have travelled to many countries to share my story of forgiveness. I have discovered that sharing my story of pain, brokenness, and forgiveness brings greater healing into my life. I learned that the first few times I shared my story, it was very painful. I was so afraid of talking about my past painful story. It saddened me.

Most of the time when I gave my talks, I could not hold back my tears. Even now, I still weep from time to time, especially when I see people in front of me weeping. I cannot hold my tears back. It is not a sign of weakness. It is healthy to cry. I have learned the secret to healing my psychological trauma in my journey. One of the symptoms of PTSD is fear. For many years after my family was killed, I was living with fears. There were a lot of fears in my life. Just seeing black uniforms frightened me. I tried to avoid seeing black uniforms. Fears actually controlled my life. They crippled my life psychologically. From a psychological point of view, fear only taught me two things—fight or flight.

Before I learned to speak in public, I was so scared. I was a very shy man. I never had the courage to talk to anyone outside of my circle. Honestly, in my youth, I never had the guts to ask a girl on a date, no matter how well I knew her. When approaching someone whom I did not know personally or had never met before, I was so nervous. My heart became frozen when I came close to them. Usually I would try my best to avoid them, unless I was left without any alternative. Then I would have to meet that person.

Standing up to speak in public was the worst fear in my life. My tongue became thicker, my mouth became dry, my face turned red, my heart pounded, and my legs were shaky. Public speaking was not my cup of tea. I was in flight mode. I did not want to tell the people about my past painful story. It made me sad all the time. When I was in flight mode, my fears controlled my life. Later, I chose to confront my internal fears by learning to tell my story. I kept reminding myself that I must not allow my fears to control me. To my surprise, the more I tell my story, the more I can control my fears. The more I give talks, the less my fears consume me. I have also learned that the more I speak in public, the more self-confidence I gain. I was a very quiet man—a man comfortable only in his own circle.

The impact of psychological trauma robbed me of my self-esteem and confidence. My confidence and self-esteem were trashed in the grave forty-two years ago. At that time, I was just a young boy, thirteen years old. I was too young to really understand what was going on in my life. I was not mature enough to handle my intellectual and emotional abilities. I could not handle my feelings. I thought my confidence and self-esteem were totally damaged beyond repair. A year after my family was killed, I lost my ability to think normally. My mind was constantly disrupted by trauma flashbacks. It took me almost thirty years, by the grace of my Shepherd, to have my confidence and self-esteem restored. It is a blessing from my Shepherd. I am forever grateful to Him for the restoration.

I previously mentioned that after my family was killed, I lost both my family and my mind. The Shepherd of my soul blessed me with substitute Mennonite families who I could depend on in my journey. They loved me and encouraged me to move on by focusing my eyes on the Cross. Eventually, my Shepherd has blessed me with my own family (my wonderful wife and two children). And my Shepherd healed my mind. Only the Shepherd of my soul can heal a broken soul like me. He is the great Physician of the soul.

In my journey of learning to cope with my life, I spent a lot of time praying to my beloved Shepherd. I asked for His mercy, healing, and restoration of my life. *"If my people, who are called by my name, will humble themselves and pray and seek my face and turn from their wicked ways, then I will hear from heaven, and I will forgive their sin and will heal their land"* (2 Chronicles 7:14). Yes, my Shepherd heard my prayers and answered them. *"Nevertheless, I will bring health and healing to it; I will heal my people and will let them enjoy abundant peace and security"* (Jeremiah 33:6).

Once I spoke to a big group of youth in a community church in Singapore. When I finished, there was time for questions and answers. Many youths asked me a lot of questions. I could answer most of them. There was one last question from a young man that gave me a big surprise, "God is good all the time. Why did God take a long time to heal you and bless you?" It was a good question. The host pastor looked at me and signaled me to wrap it up in two minutes. I joked with him, "Thank you, pastor. It took me almost thirty years to go through my journey of healing. Now, you've signaled me to wrap it up in only two minutes. It is not fair." The whole group laughed. I also laughed. God has even given me a sense of humour.

The greatest blessing in my life from the Shepherd is His healing grace. Healing can be a long journey, but sometimes it is not so. It depends on individuals, on the level of the damage they have experienced, the extent and duration of the trauma, and the age at which it happened.

I admit that I cannot give you the best answers you would expect to hear from me, but from my personal experiences, after many years of struggling with pain, depression, anxiety, nightmares, flashbacks, hopelessness, bitterness, and anger, I came to realize that my Shepherd's way of healing is a very long journey. I never got an answer from Him as to why. I hope that when I see Him personally, I will get to ask Him why He allowed me to go through such a long journey of healing.

However, as I look back over my past painful journey, I strongly believe my Shepherd allowed a long recovery because He wanted me to learn to depend on His healing grace and trust Him. He did not want me to depend on my own strategies and formulas to heal my PTSD. He did not want me to depend on the science of healing, but to depend on His healing grace.

My own strategies and formulas could never heal the broken soul; only the Shepherd of the soul could heal that. The biggest issue was whether or not I had enough patience and emotional energy to go through the long journey with my Shepherd. Learning to depend on His healing grace was never easy for me. It is also my faith in Him. Did I have enough faith in His healing grace? This is the question I asked while going through the long journey of healing. I must be honest with you. At some point in my journey, I doubted too. I cried out loudly to Him. I was wrestling with my faith too.

I have a type-A personality. I wanted quick healing. I could not wait. I did not have enough patience. I just wanted to get out of the deep, dark depression. I wanted to fix my problem quickly and get out of it. It was a test of character too. What I wanted was not what my Shepherd intended for my life. I could never learn to be still. When I could not get things done quickly, I became frustrated. Healing emotional brokenness is not as easy as healing a broken leg, where you can see the broken bones through an X-ray film. Emotional brokenness cannot be seen through an X-ray film.

In healing emotional bondage, it was always two steps forward and one step backward. The road of healing was not as smooth as I expected. I needed time and the muscle of my soul to try to pick up the shattered broken pieces and put them back together—one piece at a time. I needed a lot of time to pray for healing. I needed time to learn to listen to my Shepherd too. I needed time to count on His sufficient grace. It was an incredible journey for me, and I am grateful for the healing grace from my Shepherd.

In my journey of healing, it did not mean that I did not struggle. I am a human being like you. I went through a lot of temptations and doubts. If you examine biblical characters clearly, you will see many of them went through tons of struggles as God led them to spiritual health. God never allowed them to go through life on an easy road. For example, Abraham, Noah, Moses, Joseph, Job, David, Samuel, Isaiah, Elijah, Jeremiah, Daniel, Paul, Peter, and more.

When I had doubts, I always took time to examine these biblical heroes. In the Book of Psalms, David expressed a lot of doubts about his journey. He was angry with his Shepherd. He questioned his Shepherd. He felt hurt. He screamed out to his Shepherd for help. He felt as though his Shepherd was so far from him. But I learned one of David's secrets: he never gave up. He worked through his struggles with his Shepherd. In the end, David kept praising Him, no matter what happened to his life—he never gave up on praising him. He remained faithful to his Shepherd.

Did I get angry with my Shepherd? Did I feel disappointed with Him? Yes, I was angry with my Shepherd. I was like David. However, in wrestling with my Shepherd, I learned to scrutinize my character. In the process of my journey, I learned from the teaching of Paul through Romans 5:3-5:

> Not only so, but we also glory in our sufferings, because we know that suffering produces perseverance; perseverance, character; and character, hope. And hope does not put us to shame, because God's love has been poured out into our hearts through the Holy Spirit, who has been given to us.

Sometimes when I came across these verses, I became upset and felt despair. I could not see myself going through the process of suffering again and again. I thought that I had enough suffering in my life. I wanted to stop suffering. I wanted things to run my own way. I simply could not take it anymore. Period.

But at the same time, I knew that I failed to pick up the broken pieces to put them together. It was so terribly painful to examine my own broken pieces. Looking at them and picking them up again was the most painful process of healing. Consciously, I did not want to look at them. How could I put my broken pieces together when I did not want to pick them up? In the end, I realized that I could not escape it.

In fact, I could not escape from this process of suffering. If I were to run away from it, I would end up with another form of suffering. Predictably I would end up relying on drugs or alcohol. The drugs would have given me a quick relief—they would have made me see another world of delusion. Alcohol would have helped me suppress my painful feelings, but it would have damaged my internal organs and destroyed my family. Today, I am grateful to my Shepherd for never allowing me to fall into this deadly trap.

I have seen many Christians and church leaders who are crying out for comfort, but they do not know where to find it. When they are hit by darkness, they become confused, depressed, or disillusioned. Instead of turning themselves to seek help from their God, who is the only source of comfort, they turn to drugs to release their immediate pain. Eventually, they drift away from their God.

I have met many pastors who had been burnt out by their ministries. Church is supposed to be a place of grace. It turned out that some churches became political arenas; there were a lot of disagreements among the leaders, starting with different styles of sermons and different ways of interpreting the Bible and so on. Some leaders who did not have enough supporters among the congregation were likely kicked out of the church. Some church leaders could not cope with their difficulties and pain; they turned to drugs and alcohol to ease the pain.

They failed to learn from their experiences and did not turn to the Lord for help. In the end, they fell apart from their ministries. I felt sad to see Christian leaders falling from their ministries. One day I would like to start a ministry called, "Pastors in Pain Ministry." I would like to invite all pastors who have been hurt in their ministries to come together to share their pain and pray for healing. I know that there are many pastors and church leaders who are hurt, and are struggling to find help. I hope and pray and wait for my Shepherd's direction regarding this ministry.

When I went through my journey of wrestling with my Shepherd, I learned to accept suffering, and to cling to my Shepherd. Hardship strengthened my faith in my Shepherd. Staying apart from Him, my faith would become weak. My hardship taught me a great deal about life. It taught me to depend on my Shepherd, to trust Him deeper and deeper. Hardship produces mature faith. I captured the beauty and meaning of these verses in my life, and allowed my Shepherd to gradually mold my character. It was the journey toward my spiritual growth. He intended for me to go through the process of suffering so that I could learn to depend on Him more and more. By learning to depend on Him, I draw on His strength and receive His grace. My Shepherd gave strength to the weary:

> *He gives strength to the weary*
> *and increases the power of the weak.*
> *Even youths grow tired and weary,*
> *and young men stumble and fall;*
> *but those who hope in the LORD*
> *will renew their strength.*
> *They will soar on wings like eagles;*
> *They will run and not grow weary,*
> *they will walk and not be faint.*

(Isaiah 40:29-31)

In the deep, dark valley, my suffering produced perseverance in seeking my Shepherd. I determined that I would never give up on clinging to my Shepherd, no matter how terrible my suffering. I never stopped praying to Him. I never stopped calling for His help. I did not get a response the way I expected, but I simply did not give up. This is how my character was built up.

In the process of my suffering, I knew that my Shepherd would never leave me alone. He was there with me, and He listened to my broken heart. His voice whispered in my ears, "You can make it. Just keep moving. Don't give up. I will carry you through the journey." This whispering became the muscle of my soul. My long suffering resulted in who I am today. Out of suffering, there is hope. Hope is the most powerful muscle of my soul. Without hope, I would never have made it out of my suffering. I also knew that my faith was tested through this process of hardship and tribulation. Do you have enough patience and courage to go through this process of suffering?

Now, I know that the love and blessings of my Shepherd have been graciously poured over my life. The journey I went through and how I went through it, I now count a blessing and the joy of my life. Once I was invited to share my suffering, forgiveness, and healing from PTSD with a small group of students at the University of British Columbia. A few of these students invited their non-believer friends to come hear me. They actually wanted to expose their friends to the Christian faith. Almost at the end of my speaking, I quoted from the letter of James 1:2-4:

Consider it pure joy, my brothers and sisters, whenever you face trials of many kinds because you know that the testing of your faith produces perseverance. Let perse-

verance finish its work so that you may be mature and complete, not lacking anything.

At the end of my talk, a student organizer who managed the meeting encouraged students to ask me some questions. They gave me about thirty minutes for questions and answers. They sent all questions to the organizer. He forwarded them all to my computer. I had only thirty minutes to answer them all.

There was one question that captured my attention the most. "As I listened to your story, you went through hell in your life. You lost your whole family. You suffered from PTSD for years. After all you have gone through, how could you count it a blessing and pure joy? To me, it sounds like lunacy. Why do you count your pain and suffering as a blessing and a joy?"

The questioner did not give me his or her name. I was not sure whether he or she was a believer or not. I was not sure this questioner understood my message. I was trying to tell the students that I had a reason to rejoice in the midst of my pain and suffering, because of how my Shepherd used my suffering to build in me something so very precious, which I could never do for myself. I count it as a blessing in my life. The most important part of this blessing is that I still remain faithful to my Shepherd. I have not given up worshipping Him yet. I will forever remain faithful to Him till I meet Him eternally.

I am grateful that my Shepherd has taken me out of my darkness. Why? Because my way and my own instinct would never bring me peace. My own ability has great limitations. My Shepherd intended to mold my character and test my faith in Him. I spent many years reading many books on theological pain and suffering, philosophical and psychological pain and suffering, and sociological pain and suffering. I have read many testimonies about pain and suffering from many good Christian books. I tried my best to understand what the theologians, philosophers, psychologists, sociologists, and other people were saying about pain and suffering. I could never get a good answer. I never felt satisfied with their answers.

I have read the whole Bible more than ten times in my life, trying to dig out the best answer to the problem of pain and suffering, but I could not find a good answer. I had a lot of questions of "Why pain?" After I came through my own journey, I realized that it was not so much a question of "why," but it was the question of "to what end?" What was the outcome of my journey through the deep, dark valley of my life? What did my pain teach me in the end? As I came out of the valley, I realized I could see the meaning of life. Now, I should take my liberty to appreciate the blessings from my Shepherd. "To what end" explains how I count my experience as a blessing. To the end of my journey, will I remain faithful to my Shepherd? This is the question that I need to keep reminding myself of while I am journeying in my life.

My Shepherd has not only blessed me, but has also prepared me for helping others. I have received abundant blessings from the Shepherd of my soul. I have been set free from my bondage of bitterness, anger, pain, self-disappointment, nightmares, flashbacks, and depression. What I have learned from my journey until now I can contribute to helping others. All of these years, I have learned that the more I learn about my trials, the more I can contribute to helping others.

I feel as though my Shepherd has called me to help other people around me and around the world.

In the last twenty years, I have travelled to many different countries to speak about the message of love and forgiveness of my Shepherd. I have had the privilege of speaking at a few prison chapels in Canada. As I stood up to speak, I could see that they were all people for whom Christ has died. They failed to manage their lives. In the end, they were locked up in prison. It was a privilege to talk to some of them personally after I spoke. They told me how they ended up in prison. Some of them would have to serve at least twenty-five years, and others would have to serve less than ten years, and so on. As I listened to their stories, I learned that some of them were victims of uncontrolled anger. They were traumatized by their parents. Their psychological traumas were left untreated. In the end, they became criminals. I was so sad to hear of their pitfalls, which were preventable, but it was too late for them.

I met a very handsome young man from India, who moved to Canada with his parents when he was a little boy. His parents wanted a better life. They worked so hard on the farm. Eventually, they became rich. He grew up living a rich lifestyle. He had everything, and enjoyed the good life. One evening, when he was around nineteen years old, he could not control his anger. He said, "I pulled a trigger. I killed a young man. Now, I've ended up here for at least twenty years. I really regret what I did. I really hurt my parents the most. When I get out of here, I am not sure whether I will get to see my parents alive again. They are very old now. After I heard you speak, I will remember that you are my hero. Your message of forgiveness is so powerful. It will stay in my heart for the rest of my life."

In the end, he asked me to pray for him. After I prayed, he asked for my permission to give me a hug. He was weeping while hugging me. I gave him my book, *After the Heavy Rain*. He asked for my email address. He said, "Pastor, when I get out of this place, I will email you." It has been almost ten years now. I hope to hear from him one day.

I have helped to set some people free. In my deep, dark valley of life, my Shepherd was there preparing me to help others and calling me to that ministry. Paul said:

> *Praise be to the God and Father of our Lord Jesus Christ, the Father of compassion and the God of all comfort, who comforts us in all our troubles so that we can comfort those in any trouble with the comfort we ourselves receive from God. For just as we share abundantly in the sufferings of Christ, so also our comfort abounds through Christ.*

> *If we are distressed, it is for your comfort and salvation; if we are comforted, it is for your comfort, which produces in you patient endurance of the same sufferings we suffer. And our hope for you is firm because we know that just as you share in our sufferings, so also you share in our comfort* (2 Corinthians 1:3-7).

The word "missionary" never existed in my vocabulary when I was young. I never knew what it meant until I came to Canada and became a Christian. I heard a missionary who came to share in my church about his ministry in Africa. It never occurred to me that I might be a missionary. Even though I went to study at Christian schools,

I had never wanted to be a missionary. I recalled when I was in my last years at seminary, there was a Mission Fest at the school. I spoke to many missionaries at the Mission Fest. They asked me, "Will you go to serve the Lord in your country after you finish your studies?" My instant response was "NO."

I was so scared to return to my country. I thought I could never have the courage to face my own pain. I recalled the last promise I made in front of the grave that I would never come back to Cambodia. A few years after I finished my studies at Providence Seminary, my Shepherd led me through the journey of my suffering, and comforted me to comfort others. I learned one lesson in my life—I should never underestimate what the Shepherd of my soul could do in my life.

In the last twenty years of my ministry in Cambodia, I had lots of opportunities to help others when they were in the deep, dark valleys of their lives. Besides Cambodia, I have travelled to many countries to speak about my pain, suffering, and forgiveness to others. I have found that sharing what I have learned through trials is helpful in helping others. The deeper I face my own brokenness, the more effectively I can help others. One of my professors once said to me, "Reaksa, you will have the greatest impact when people see how you have gone through the valley of the shadow of death, faith intact." My own personal experience has proven to be an effective tool, not for my head knowledge, but for heart knowledge.

I was invited to speak at a church in Australia. After I finished speaking, a lady approached me. She politely asked me if she could give me a hug. After giving me a hug, she asked to speak to me personally. I sat down with her. When I looked into her eyes, I could tell that she was depressed, confused, and lost. She could hardly speak, tears pouring down her face. She was choked up emotionally, but she tried to express what was troubling her. "This does not make sense to me. I can't imagine how you dealt with it. I don't understand how you could get out of your darkness and bitterness. How can you share your terrible painful story?" I did not say anything to her. I just wanted to let her have her own time to release her tears. I patiently listened to her.

She continued, "I have been coming to this church for almost two years now. I have not decided to accept the Lord yet. But after hearing your story and how the Lord led you out of your deep darkness, depression, and bitterness, I want a change. You went to forgive your enemy. And how the Lord healed you. Will you pray for me?"

I politely asked her, "How can I pray for you?"

"I want to forgive my husband who has abused me for many years. And I want to accept Jesus Christ as my Lord and Saviour now."

As soon as I heard her prayer requests, I decided to call her pastor and a few elders of the church to come to pray for her and lead her to the Lord. We laid hands on her and prayed for her, while she continued to cry so loudly. She surrendered her life to the Lord. He filled her heart with joy as she entered into the family of God. It was a special privilege for me to be able to help her. In the last twenty years, I have had the joy of helping many other people through my sharing. I could write many more stories of my experiences of meeting people.

Being a missionary is not natural for me, but the amazing grace of my Shepherd prepared me to return to my homeland, where I once promised I would never step back for the rest of my life, to meet my enemies, forgive them, and bless them. I realized that the people in that village had never been properly educated. There was no school in the village. They were still living in a primitive way and would be trapped in poverty for many generations to come. My heart was filled with compassion for them. This wasn't an easy love for me, but I felt as though my Shepherd had called me to take another step forward in helping them. I have received a lot of blessings from my Shepherd. Now, I needed to pass these blessings to others. They would know that I am a follower of Jesus Christ by my love for them. It was a big challenge, but the love of my Shepherd compelled me to do it.

After my first book, *Tears of my Soul* was published, I travelled to promote my book in other countries. I sold some books, and collected enough funds to cover the cost of building a school with two classrooms. I went back to the village to bless the people there with a school. A few years later, with the help of Ratanak International, I was able to add two more classrooms and a library. I kept adding more books for the library and also provided school uniforms and sports team uniforms for the students. I also brought medical teams from Singapore, Canada, and the USA to come to do medical check-ups of the people in this village.

On October 1, 2004, the school was dedicated to the use of the village people. More than 200 came for this special dedication, and my heart was filled with mixed emotions—happiness and sadness. I was happy to see what I had done for the people in this village, even though it was, humanly speaking, impossible. I would never have dreamt of doing such a thing, but the grace of my Shepherd motivated me to finish this formidable mission. I was invited to give a speech for the school dedication. I inserted this speech in my second book, *After the Heavy Rain*. Now, I would like to use it again for this book.

"Good morning. It is a special privilege for me to be with you this morning. It is good to be back to see many old friends and to meet others whom I do not recognize at all. First of all, I want to thank God for sparing my life. God has a special purpose for me to bring you a message of forgiveness today. Before I make my address, let me assure you again that it is God's grace that brings me back here today, and I thank God so much for this special day.

"I have heard that many people in the village have been speculating that I was building this school in order to express my gratitude and pay respect to my family. Others have been speculating that I am trying to build up merit points in this life so that I will be intelligent in the next one. Now, I'd like you to allow me to explain that none of these speculations are correct. I have built this school for two reasons. Firstly, this school is a symbol of my forgiveness to the people in this village, and I believe you are aware of what happened to my family more than twenty years ago. They were killed here, but I survived the execution, and I thank God for sparing my life.

"Do you know how I felt after my family was killed? I lived with painful memories that could never have been forgotten. I have experienced trauma, nightmares, and depression. When I was in the grave, I had no hope that I would have a day like this. But God took me from the grave and restored my life. He has taken me on a long, painful journey back here to deal with this unwanted emotional

278

legacy. It took me many years to learn to forgive and it was very hard. I never thought that I could return to this village with a blessing for you, but God has a special mission for me.

"Do you know the reason I decided to name this school 'God's Grace Primary School?' This is to serve as a reminder that I am alive today because of God's grace in my life. It is not my own fortune [or *bonn*, meaning merited credit] that saved me. Rather, it is absolutely God's grace. The moment I was hit from behind and fell into the grave with many other victims is beyond many people's imagination. If God had not saved me that day, I might have been buried alive; I might not have had the chance to speak to you today. God's grace is so amazing. What God has done in my life is truly a work of His amazing grace. Only that grace would enable me to forgive you and bless you with this school. This blessing is born out of God's grace, not my generous heart. You know this act of forgiveness and blessing would be impossible at a human level, but it is possible with God.

"It is not easy to learn to forgive. For some of you, if someone steals something from you, even just a small thing, what you often do is pick up your ax in order to chase and kill the thief. This is a common practice here in this village. You are not able to forgive even a small thing. But my whole family was butchered in front of me. How do you think I felt? Yet despite the hurt, bitterness, and anger, I have learned to forgive. Frankly, years ago, I longed to take revenge for my family. I could not forget the first promise I had made in front of my family's grave.

"Some of you were aware that I was a policeman in the city. A few of you have mentioned to me that you did not have the courage to go to the city, because you were afraid of me. I will be very honest with you. If I had seen you while I was a policeman, I would have killed you all. At that time, I was deeply influenced by the pursuit of family honour—revenge was my top priority.

"But many years after I had become a Christian, God helped me to learn to forgive. First, He forgave my countless sins, and then He helped me to set myself free from the bondage of bitterness. It is morally right for me to forgive you. Forgiveness was given as a gift from God for me. Now, I would like to pass on this gift of God to you. This school is my symbol of forgiveness for you. It is a blessing from a Christian brother and part of the history of forgiveness in this village. I believe that none of you can do this yet, but if you are angry with someone, or if someone wrongs or hurts you in any way, please remember my example of forgiveness. Please do not kill any more innocent people. Please learn to live with each other in peace and harmony.

"Secondly, I built this school for you and for your children. I would like your children to move out of the bondage of poverty and have a better life. I would like them to learn how to read. I strongly believe that education brings a better understanding of life. My late father used to teach me, 'A man without knowledge will always be brought down by what he does not understand.' It will help your children to move out of this primitive culture. I want to see your children living not with blood on their hands, but in peaceful harmony with each other.

"What I would like to see in the future is that some of the children who come to study in this school, ten to fifteen years from now, will come back to teach here. I would like to see a bright future for your children in the next generation. Please do not forget to remind your children that this school is a symbol of forgiveness from a Christian brother who lost his family in this village, and who chose to forgive instead of taking revenge.

"Jesus said, 'Love your enemies, do good to those who hate you, speak well of those who speak badly of you and pray for those who abuse you' (Luke 6:27–28). This is the most important teaching in the Christian life. This school is the symbol of my forgiveness and, through it, I demonstrate my love to you. It is the grace of God that has transformed my hatred into love. I never thought I could accomplish this difficult task. I am just a simple human being like you; I feel weak. I must sincerely confess to you that I do not have the emotional energy to turn hatred into love, but God has given me the strength to achieve this. I know that nothing is impossible with God.

"Before I end my speech this morning, may I ask you to take care of this school? I am not asking you to do it for me, but for yourselves; it is not my school, but yours. Please keep it well maintained.

"A Christian sister who has contributed funds to help build this school sends her word of encouragement to you. She gives her greetings and hearty congratulations to you. Her prayer for you is that you will be much blessed by the teaching that you will receive at the school and that you will be able to understand and experience God's love for you. She wishes that you will cherish and protect the school and do your best to make sure that only good things are taught here, and that it will be used only for good things. Every time you see the school, may you remember that Jesus loves you very much.

"Once again, thank you so much for giving me an opportunity to speak to you this morning. May this school be a blessing to your children, generation after generation. May God richly bless you all."

In the last few years, I have heard that some of the kids who went to this school went on to become teachers, nurses, and IT technicians; one former student is in medical school, and two others are in law school. My heart is filled with great joy. In my current hometown of Pouk, I have been able to bless the community with a community centre, a local library, computer lessons, a church, community roads, drainage systems, physical education programs, a football field, hockey, badminton, pickle ball courts, a children's playground, student dorms, scholarship programs for poor students, and several more community projects. I have left a good legacy for the community.

I am so happy about the scholarship program for poor students. This is the story of how it was established. I went to have my hair cut by a local barber. He was a local man. While waiting for my turn, I heard the man who was having his hair cut talking to the barber about his childhood experience. He told the barber that he was raised in a very poor family. Then I heard him mention my father's name. His father could not afford to send him to school, but wanted him to work on the farm. My father knew his father. My father went to his father and asked if he could support him to go to school. His father was very happy. My father gave him money to go to school, until the country fell to the communists in 1975. After that, he never heard from my father again. He was not aware that I was the son of the man he was talking about. I just listened to his story with heartfelt joy. I did not need to say anything to him. My father left a great legacy for this man. This story resonated in my heart forever.

Then a God-ordained event occurred. I heard a pastor preach about giving and how he came to know the Lord. He told a story of a missionary family (a couple with five kids) who went to serve in India. For some unexpected reason, the man died. He left behind his spouse and his five kids. The mission committee in the USA raised about $2000.00 to relocate the family to the USA. The wife decided not to take the money, but gave it to the mission organization in India, because they needed the money more than her family did. The mission organization used the money to support the local workers to travel to the countryside to bring the Good News to others. It happened that the preacher and his brother-in-law became Christians as a result of her giving money to the Lord. This story touched my heart profoundly. The next morning, I got a letter from Phil Parshall. In the letter, there was a check for US$2,000.00 made out to me and a note:

Dear Reaksa,

The Lord told me that you need money for your family. This is a small amount of money from our retirement savings. May the Lord bless your family.

Phil and Julie Parshall

The amount of money was exactly the same amount as in the pastor's story. I took this as a word from my Shepherd. It was true that I did not have enough money for my family. In fact, I had just flown back from Cambodia to prepare for the arrival of my first-born son,

Philos. In my bank account, I had only US$450.00. I did not have a place to stay. My family was blessed by the mercy and kindness of Margaret Gilligan and Ron Apperley for allowing us to stay in their house. I also owed about C$40,000 in Canadian student loans. I was desperate for money to help my family and pay back the bank. I received US$2,000.00 from Phil Parshall.

I told my wife that I felt the Lord was directing me to use this money to set up a scholarship funds for the poor students in Cambodia. I shared my idea of setting up scholarship funds for poor students with many good friends who also chipped in. I have been able to fund more than ten students to go to local universities. Most of the scholarship recipients graduated from IT, English, and banking programs. I am happy that I can make a small contribution to impact the Cambodian society.

Many local authorities in my hometown where I grew up have appreciated what I have done for the community. Once I sat down with the local governor. He asked me a very good question. "Brother, I have seen a lot of people coming back to Cambodia, but you came back to help the community. Other people came back for their personal gain and fame. But you are different. You came back to help the community. Our people have observed your behaviour. You are so different. You don't drink with us. You don't hang around with girls. You only speak about the love of your God. You have done so many community projects here, and you keep telling us about the love of your God. What do you really want?" I knew this governor personally. He was very honest with me. He broke his silence by asking what I actually wanted. I was so surprised to hear that from him. I simply told him, "My philosophy of life is very simple. If I can make someone smile, I will be happy."

He responded, "On behalf of the local authorities, we want to thank you for what you have done for the community. You have indeed made the whole community smile. Some farmers in this area are so happy. You have been leaving a good legacy for this community."

I am forever grateful for my Shepherd who has blessed me and has called me to bless others. It was a special privilege for me to be able to serve in this community. Without my Shepherd, I could not have done anything.

Jesus said:

"I am the vine; you are the branches. If you remain in me and I in you, you will bear much fruit; apart from me, you can do nothing. If you do not remain in me, you are like a branch that is thrown away and withers; such branches are picked up, thrown into the fire and burned" (John 15:5-6).

PRAYER:

Lord, Shepherd of my soul. You are my Provider, and my Defender. I am grateful to You for sparing my life and for saving me from the grave. You have brought me a long way from the grave to Canada. Now, You have brought me back to the country where I had made a promise that I would never come back for the rest of my life. Now, I have an opportunity to serve You in this country. Thank you for blessing me and preparing me to come back. When I first came back, it was very painful for me, but You healed my brokenness through my journey. Thank You for blessing me abundantly. Now, I can pass on my blessings to others.

Shepherd of my soul, without You, I can do nothing. Thank you for giving me a special privilege to bless others. Amen.

I would like to conclude with a Psalm of thanksgiving from King David:

> Give thanks to the LORD, for he is good;
> his love endures forever.
> Let the redeemed of the LORD tell their story—
> those he redeemed from the hand of the foe,
> those he gathered from the lands,
> from east and west, from north and south.
> Some wandered in desert wastelands,
> finding no way to a city where they could settle.
> They were hungry and thirsty, and their lives ebbed away.
> Then they cried out to the Lord in their trouble,
> and he delivered them from their distress.
> He led them by a straight way
> to a city where they could settle.
> Let them give thanks to the Lord for his unfailing love
> and his wonderful deeds for mankind,
> for he satisfies the thirsty
> and fills the hungry with good things.

(Psalm 107:1-9)

YOUR REVIEW & REFLECTION

1. Have you ever been blessed by your Shepherd? Write about it down below:

2. Do you think that your Shepherd has been good to you? Write it down.

3. Do you love your Shepherd? In what way?

4. Do you want to bless others? In what way(s)?

5. Write one way you want to bless others.

6. Who needs your blessing in their life? How can you pass that blessing on to them in a way that is genuine and appropriate for them?

7. What unique gift do you have that can be a blessing to others?

8. Write your prayers:

CONCLUSION

Once, I was invited to speak at Seattle Pacific University. At the end of my talk, one student asked me, "Pastor, is PTSD curable?" I was reluctant to answer her question. From my studies, clinically, I have learned that PTSD is not curable, but it is treatable, and manageable. There is a lot of debate about whether PTSD can be cured. I personally do not believe that it can be cured. I have not seen any scientific literature that has indicated that PTSD can be cured. I have not heard a psychologist or psychiatrist who claims that PTSD can be cured. From a psychological point of view, there is a strong possibility those symptoms of PTSD might return.

I did not want her to lose hope with what I had to say. PTSD can be treated. There are some special counselling and therapeutic approaches that can help PTSD sufferers to learn to cope with the symptoms of PTSD. Several therapeutic approaches such as behavioural and cognitive therapies, exposure therapy, eye movement desensitization and reprocessing (EMDR), narrative exposure therapy, group therapy, and more. In addition to these therapies, medication is also a helpful treatment for the symptoms of PTSD, such as depression, anxiety disorders, and insomnia.

Please be aware that medication alone is not the best solution for the treatment of PTSD, but it can be useful for PTSD sufferers to cope with their depression, anxiety disorders, and insomnia for a short period of time. Medication can help patients to be able to adjust, but it can never heal psychological trauma. I think that for a short-term effect, medication is helpful for dealing with depression, anxiety disorders, and insomnia. I used to take antidepressant medication. I went to see a doctor who prescribed me antidepressants for a month. It helped me to sleep better. After I finished taking it for a month, I could not sleep. I went back to the doctor. He gave me one more month's worth of antidepressants.

After that, I realized that I was on the road to depending on the antidepressants. I could not sleep without them. I finally decided to stop taking them. While taking an antidepressant, I learned that I had some troubles with side-effects such as tiredness, dry mouth, and constipation. It helped me to sleep better, but I felt so tired in the morning. I lost my motivation to get up in the early morning. I just wanted to sleep more. For myself, I decided not to continue on antidepressant medication, but I have no objection to it. I have met many Christian friends who took antidepressant medication for years. This was just my experience with medication. I was strongly determined to seek healing from my Shepherd. I needed to learn to depend on the amazing grace of my Shepherd to move through my journey of healing my emotional and psychological wounds.

Meditation is a mental discipline. I learned to contemplate on the Scriptures—picturing myself in the Word of my Shepherd. Learning how to be still and contemplate on the Word of my Shepherd was a big challenge. It took me many years to learn to be still. Learning to meditate on Psalm 23, I came to the conviction that the most important thing about my meditation was my mind, and the most important thing about my mind was how I fixed my mind on the Shepherd of my soul. I must honestly admit that it was not as easy as it sounded. I am not a robot. I am a human being. There was a time I was facing many challenges, and my mind derailed from my Shepherd. I was angry. I was disappointed. I was restless. I was distracted by flashbacks. Sometimes, I felt as though my Shepherd was far from me. Several times in my journey of learning to meditate on the Scriptures, I almost gave up. But I always tried my best to come back to my Shepherd by confessing my failure to fix my mind on Him. I came to my Shepherd to ask Him to grant me strength to deal with my own failure. I consciously chose to remain with my Shepherd by redirecting my mind to Him. "Set your minds on things above, not on earthly things (Colossians 3:2). The Lord is my Shepherd and in Him I find my security and serenity. Meditation, for me, is the art of learning to control my mind, and learning to discern the Word of my Shepherd. After years of learning to meditate through Psalm 23, my flashbacks and nightmares vanished from me.

I cannot explain from a scientific perspective why my meditation on Psalm 23 helped me to overcome my symptoms of PTSD. I cannot explain why my flashbacks and nightmares vanished from me through my meditation.

From a spiritual point of view, one thing I can simply conclude is that the Shepherd of my soul healed my broken soul. "Apart from me, you can do nothing" (John 15:5). He restored my life after many years of struggling with the symptoms of PTSD. I am a living testimony that my Shepherd healed my broken spirit. He set me free from the bondage of nightmares and flashbacks.

The healing of my personal psychological trauma has taken me through a long journey—a slow journey to maturity. There was no shortcut on the road to healing. I went through a lot of journeys through deep, dark valleys. I know what it meant. I had not only been wrestling with symptoms of PTSD, but I had also been wrestling with my spiritual battle as well. Through the eyes of Psalm 23, I could see the beauty of healing grace for my life again. Meditation on Psalm 23 helped me learn to surrender to my Shepherd. I felt secure in my sleep as I meditated on the Scriptures. It was a spiritual healing. It also helped me to build up my self-esteem and confidence. Through meditation, I have discovered the art of learning to control my restless mind. And it helped me deal with my own symptoms of PTSD.

As I look back over the journey of my life from the grave to Canada, I am grateful to my Shepherd that He has taken me on a long journey through the deep, dark valley of my life to see His amazing grace. Eventually, the Shepherd of my soul took me back to visit the grave again. There are no words to possibly express my gratitude to the Shepherd of my soul for sparing my life from the grave and restoring my life. Now, I can smile again. It has been a long, painful journey for me. But I now can see blessing and healing grace in my life as a result!

I have travelled to speak at a number of churches, schools, Christian organizations, prisons, and small groups, and participated in television and radio interviews. People often asked me this simple question, "How do you cope or deal with your psychological trauma?" Gaining knowledge of PTSD was very helpful for me. After I realized that I suffered from PTSD, I dedicated my life to researching it to gain a broader perspective on the impact of psychological trauma. It helped me to understand my behaviours and how I relived my trauma. Basic knowledge of PTSD helped me understand my struggles. Gaining an understanding of the impact of PTSD was very helpful for me, but living through the symptoms of PTSD myself gave me tons of experience. When sitting down with someone suffering from PTSD, I can clearly understand his or her struggles with the symptoms of PTSD.

Besides trying to understand the impact of PTSD, I kept journals. In fact, this book is born out of more than thirty years of my life. Writing my own journals was very helpful for me in examining my brokenness, anger, bitterness, disappointment, hurt, nightmares, flashbacks, and depression. It also helped me to keep my memories alive. After I became a Christian, I learned to pray to the Shepherd of my soul to help me deal with my symptoms of PTSD. I learned that my Shepherd never answered my prayer immediately. In the midst of my struggles, I felt disappointed with Him—where was He when I needed Him the most? I learned to wait. Having a type-A personality like me, however, learning to wait was a big challenge. I often lost my patience. It produced doubts. I learned that doubts were normal, but that my Shepherd would never leave me to drift away from Him or let me lose my focus on the Cross. I learned to call out to Him more and more to depend on His amazing grace. To be still and know that the Lord is the Shepherd of my soul. It was a blessed journey for me.

Telling my story to others is the healthiest way of dealing with my PTSD. When I tell the story to others, I feel as though I can release a sense of victimization—I am no longer a victim and I am no longer chained in the deep, dark valley of the past. I can overcome my fear. As a shy man, public speaking was not my cup of tea; it was just not my way of life. I did not have the courage to stand up in front of big audiences to speak to people. However, all these years, the Shepherd of my soul has taught me to face my fears by telling my story. Telling my story to others is a part of overcoming my psychological trauma. I could release it even though I had to relive my painful personal experiences. In psychology, we call it self-desensitization. Telling the story does not only help me to release my psychological trauma, but it also helps me to overcome my fears.

I mentioned earlier about the fight-or-flight mode. When I was in the flight mode, my fears controlled me— my psychological trauma was uncontrollably repeated in my mind again and again, reinforcing the cycle of fear. Telling my story is partly healing me from my psychological trauma. In psychology, we say "talking is healing." Actually, after speaking in public so many times, I have regained my confidence and self-esteem.

While serving as a missionary in my hometown in Pouk district in Siem Reap Province, I hosted many teams from YMCA Singapore. Most of the teams were students from high schools, colleges, and universities. They came to do some work for the community. The team leader, Andrew Leo, always asked me to tell my story to the students.

One young student asked me, "Pastor Reaksa, did you ever seek help from a psychologist or psychiatrist when you were in Canada?"

I responded to her, "No. In Canada, in my early Christian faith, I would never trust anyone. I could not bring myself to trust someone I didn't know. I did not want to tell someone of my mental health problem. I did not want people to know what was going on in my mind."

She continued to ask, "How did you cope with your psychological trauma and how did you learn to trust other people?"

I answered, "It is a very good question. It took a long time. After I realized that I suffered from PTSD, I dedicated myself to studying the impact and the consequences of PTSD. At one point, I thought that I should seek help from mental health professionals, but I could not afford to pay for the therapy. It was very expensive. But the biggest barrier for me was that I did not trust other people. It was foolish to pay for therapy when I could not trust someone.

"Later, I learned to talk to myself. I wrote the questions. I sat down in front of a mirror, and I asked myself some questions such as,

"'Reaksa, tell me what was happening with you when the Khmer Rouge took you to the jungle.' 'How did you feel when you saw them kill your father?' 'And many more questions.'"

After they heard my questions, some students were laughing. I had no idea why they were laughing. I told them, "In fact, it was very painful to sit down in front of the mirror, look into my face and learn to answer these questions. Do you know why it was painful for me? The first few times, I bravely tried to face the reality of deep hurt inside me, but I could never bring myself to answer these questions. I could not bring myself to see my face in the mirror. Painful memories resurfaced in my mind. It was very painful for me to handle my traumatic memories. However, it helped me to cry in front of the mirror. Did you ever look at yourself in the mirror when you cry? I can tell you that it looked terribly ugly. It took me a few years to learn to talk to myself in the mirror. It may sound a bit crazy to you, but I learned a secret thing through this process. I learned to trust myself. It was a new journey for me. It helped me to open an avenue to build up trust with others. It was very difficult, but I learned to build up my trust and confidence. I had the courage to speak to myself about my pain inside my heart. I tried to speak out instead of suppressing it in my chest. The more I talked to myself in the mirror, the more confidence I gained."

I was not so sure these students could comprehend what I was telling them, but I could tell that they were interested in listening to me. My journey of healing emotional and psychological wounds was very uncomfortable and painful. It required much emotional energy to rely on the grace of the Shepherd of my soul to bring me from emotional bondage to freedom. I have learned that meditation and prayer are the most effective way of healing. I realized that in the deep, dark valley of my life, I needed to rely on the Shepherd of my soul. He helped me to walk through my journey once I acknowledged my dependency on my Shepherd. Meditating on the Word of my Shepherd and talking to Him through my prayers helped me to realize that He walked with me in the journey. It helped me to stay close to my Shepherd. It also helped me to realize that His love endures forever.

The Lord is close to the brokenhearted and saves those who are crushed in spirit (Psalm 34:18).

My Shepherd had saved me and delivered me from the deep, dark valley. Now, I am able to feel normal again.

People commonly asked me this question, "Do you still have nightmares and flashbacks?" Thankfully, by the grace of my Shepherd, I have not had any nightmares or flashbacks since 1997. The Shepherd of my soul has cast my nightmares and flashbacks from me. Since then, I have not seen myself being chased by the Khmer Rouge soldiers or the Canadian police again. The concept of hatred of the black uniforms melted away from me. I have bought many black T-shirts and black clothes. With that being resolved, the only remaining problem related to my PTSD is my chest pain.

Once I called my doctor friend. She is a well-respected medical doctor. She picked up the phone and said, "Good morning, Reaksa. What makes you call me in the early morning?" I told her that I had had some chest pain for one week. In trying to figure out what was wrong with me, she asked me many questions related to my chest pain, cardiac history, and so on. After fifteen minutes on the phone, she suggested that I should go to a heart specialist soon. From her diagnosis, it was an early sign of heart attack. She suggested that I get myself checked out, and the sooner the better.

Every year, especially in late November, I would have chest pain for at least two weeks. After that, the pain in my chest subsided by itself. I went to see a few doctors and told them about my pain. Doctors initially thought that the pain in my chest was an early sign of heart attack. They sent me for all kinds of tests from MRIs, CAT scans, chest x-rays, and ECGs, but they could not find anything wrong with my heart. They were puzzled by my chest pain. One doctor in Thailand was surprised when I told her that I had been having chest pain for at least forty years. After she conducted all the tests again, she could not find anything abnormal in my heart. All the reports she obtained from the computer showed no sign of blockage. She did not understand why I had been having chest pain for so long. In the end, she did not know what to suggest to me.

Many years after that, I learned that my chest pain was associated with the anniversary of the traumatic event that took place in late November 1977. I realized that by the end of November, I felt the loss of my whole family creeping into my heart. I just felt some kind of sadness. I just wanted to grieve for losing my family. I believe that after that tragedy in my life, my body and my mind encoded some kinds of psychosomatic symptoms. Chest pain arrives on cue. I would call it a psychological clock encoded in my body and mind. When the psychological clock reached November, the anniversary of the execution of my family, it sent a signal to my heart and I would feel pain in my chest. The pain was not so serious, but it was a bit of discomfort. The cycle of pain repeats itself every November. I think that my body is carrying memories of trauma. I wish I could offer a clear scientific explanation of my chest pain, but I could not find a better explanation. I can only surmise that my chest pain in late November is part of the symptoms of PTSD. Please note that this is my personal experience. This psychological clock is not included as a symptom in the DSM-V. I just want to share this from my personal experience.

Even after all these years, I cannot turn back the psychological clock. I cannot erase the anniversary of the traumatic event in my life. However, I have learned one thing—my chest pain constantly reminds me not to victimize others. I am still learning to accept what has happened in my life. I need to rely on the Shepherd of my soul to move on day by day. Life after tragedy is a matter of learning how to deal with grief, sorrow, and pain.

The more I learn about grief, sorrow, and pain, the more I become aware that I need to depend on the grace of the Shepherd of my soul. When I reach late November every year, I keep reminding myself that the grace of my Shepherd is sufficient for me. It has been forty-three years since my family was killed. I cannot change the clock of the anniversary of my tragedy, but I will learn to live with it by depending on the strength of my Shepherd.

For what you have done
I will always praise you
in the presence of your faithful people.
And I will hope in your name, for your name is good.

(Psalm 52:9)

Other than the chest pain every November, symptoms of PTSD such as nightmares, flashbacks, and depression are no longer disturbing me. I am grateful to the Shepherd of my soul. He has taken me on a long journey from the deep darkness to freedom. It has been a long journey for me to go through. Now, I can see the beauty of blessing from my Shepherd. Many years of consistent meditation helped me to overcome my PTSD. Meditation and prayer are very powerful tools to deal with PTSD. I could never have imagined that I could overcome my PTSD. My Shepherd has cleaned my traumatized mind, and He filled me with a new spirit. He guided me and empowered me to use my own personal experiences to help others who are broken.

In my Shepherd, I find my deepest security, and my needs are met. All I need is to learn to surrender to my Shepherd, day by day.

In my Shepherd, I find peace, serenity, and tranquility. My spirit is renewed. All I need is to learn to trust my Shepherd, and allow Him to guide me.

In my Shepherd, I find meaning in life, and He restores my health and my family. All I need is to allow Him to restore me and mold me according to His purpose.

In my Shepherd, I find my courage in the deep darkness of the valley of life. Courage is not the absence of fear, but the presence of my Shepherd with me. All I need is to walk with Him and allow Him to navigate me through the deep, dark valley of my life.

In my Shepherd, I find a special honour in Him, and my Shepherd anoints my head with oil. All I need is to acknowledge His love and His faithfulness for my life.

In my Shepherd, I find my blessings, and my Shepherd calls me to bless others. All I need is to bring the blessing to others and to live my life to shine for my Shepherd.

Your Summary

Please take a moment to reflect through your life and write down six points to share in your small group about what you have learned from this book.

GLOSSARY

Angkar	organization
angkar loeu	higher organization
bong	older brother or sister
chao	grandson or granddaughter
chlop	Khmer Rouge secret agent or investigator
Khmer Rouge	Khmer Communist, Red Khmer
khmang	enemy
mak	mother
mith	comrade
new-liberated people	those who lived in the cities or outside the Khmer Rouge's zones before the country was liberated in April 17, 1975, also called "17th of April's people"
old-liberated people	those who lived in the Khmer Rouge's zones before the country was liberated in April 17, 1975
pa or papa	father
pook	father
ta or tata	elder, elderly (male)
sent to school or to study	to be executed

About the Author

Sokreaksa (Reaksa) Himm is the author of *The Tears of my Soul*, which describes his journey to freedom, faith, and purpose, and *After the Heavy Rain*, which tells of his journey to forgiveness of and reconciliation with the people who killed his family.

In his book, *Shepherd of My Soul,* he describes his journey from the deep, dark valley of his life to recovery. Life after a major loss is a matter of learning how to cope with emotional and psychological crises and trauma (PTSD). The more he learns about his own emotional and psychological crises, the more he becomes aware of his need to depend on the sufficient grace of the Good Shepherd to heal his PTSD.

Reaksa and his wife, Sophaly Eng, have two children—Philos and Sophia—and together spent twenty years serving as missionaries in Cambodia. They returned to Toronto in 2019.

Reaksa is an international speaker. He has travelled to many countries to share his experience of pain and forgiveness. Reaksa can be reached via email at reaksashepherdofmysoul@gmail.com, or his website, www.theshepherdofmysoul.com.

CPSIA information can be obtained at www.ICGtesting.com
Printed in the USA
BVHW040604121021
618721BV00003B/6

9 781460 013304